Common Cents:

Stretch Every Dollar

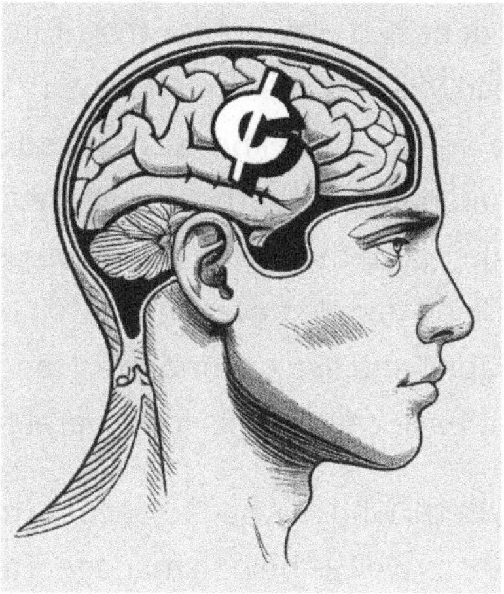

Dedication

Thanks to my mom (Bonnie), Dad (Joe), and grandparents, Ralph and Maxine. They all worked hard, took care of all of our necessities, saved, and lived below their means. They structured their lives to use common sense to stay out of debt and prepare for their future and ultimate retirement. They lived low-stress lives and always maintained reserves (emergency funds) so no surprise expenses caused additional stress. I've learned many helpful habits from them that are filtered throughout this book to help readers find that more peaceful, confident financial place in life. I've seen many people never reach that place because they have developed bad habits and live beyond their means. The pandemic conditions seem to have caused this for several people I know.

Thanks also to my wife, Beth, who has had to become much more familiar with our financial picture as well as help to manage it as it has grown. She got a huge wake-up call when I ate the pavement in a pickleball match with a heart attack and flatlined years ago (see Action 9). She has learned a lot about all of the facets by continually adding to her knowledge. She has also learned by, once again, being my Editor-In-Chief of this new book. She went through every piece, leaving me lots of red-lined paragraphs, most of which I adopted to make this better. Even though we were both Law Review writers and editors in law school, she is the stronger editor, which I (and you will) appreciate. A good, quality book doesn't happen without strong professionals like her. I just happen to have an inside track.

Special recognition to my little buddies and closest canine friends, Katie and Lexi (our Bichon-Maltese sisters), who were sleeping, playing, eating, singing, and barking in my office and throughout the house each day as I learned these concepts and I put this together. Their company helps improve my demeanor when I miss the interactions with coworkers I used to get at a "regular" job.

This is also dedicated to those readers that actually go through the process and change their own financial lives because they took action. Make these actions new habits and you'll continue to achieve goals bigger than you think are possible now.

Common Cents:

Stretch Every Dollar

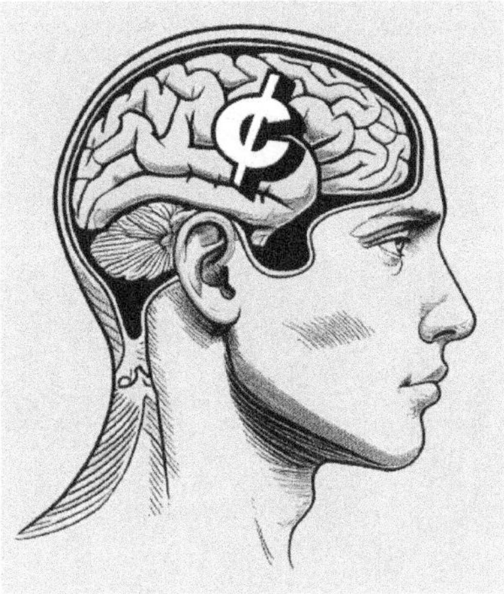

Become An Expense Assassin:

A. Slash Costs

B. Increase Net Income

C. Reduce Worry

Jeff Wilson, MBA, CMA, JD

Table of Actions

Prestige Publishing books may be purchased for educational, business, or sales promotional use in bulk. For details about this program, email Jeff at the address below "Attn: Bulk Sales." Or call toll free at 1-866-475-4675.

Prestige Publishing
A Division of Prestige Media Group, LLC
Toledo, OH 43617
Ph: 419-842-8112
Email: jeff@lifescheatsheets.com

Printed in the United States of America
Book Cover and Layout design by: Prestige Publishing, a Division of Prestige Media Group, LLC
Copy Editors: Beth A. (Rowe) Wilson, JD, Hemingway, Grammarly

ISBN-13: 978-0-9845965-1-5

Disclaimer and Legal Notice

Throughout this book, you will need to consider all of the other factors in your life at that time to make the best decision for your particular situation. The author has given suggestions based on typical circumstances, but if your situation is different, change your decisions accordingly. Use this information as you see fit and at your own risk. Readers are urged to consult a variety of sources and educate themselves about these areas before taking any risks. The advice and strategies contained herein may not be suitable for every case.

Please remember that the information in this book may be subject to varying state and local laws or regulations that may apply to the user's particular situation. Adherence to all applicable laws and regulations, federal, state, and local, and all other aspects of doing business in the U.S. or any other jurisdiction, is the sole responsibility of the reader.

All trademarks such as eBay.com, Amazon.com, etc., service marks, product names, and company names are assumed to be the property of their respective owners, and are used only for reference. There is no implied endorsement by those entities. Likewise, the fact that an organization or website is referenced in this work as a potential source of further information does not mean that the author or the publisher endorses, has confirmed, or warrants the information provided in this book or in those references.

This book is sold with the understanding that the author and publisher are not engaged in rendering legal, accounting, tax, or other professional services with this book (especially for less than $20). There is no engagement agreement, no attorney-client relationship, and no other professional relationship with you. If legal, accounting, or other expert assistance is required, you should seek the services of a competent professional to assist you.

The author and publisher make no representations or warranties with respect to the accuracy or completeness of the contents of this work and specifically disclaim all warranties, express or implied, including without limitation warranties of fitness for a particular purpose or merchantability. No warranty may be created or extended by sales or promotional materials.

Please note that much of this publication is based on personal experience and represents the opinions of the author as of the date of publication. The author and publisher shall in no event be held liable to any party for any direct, indirect, punitive, special, incidental, or other consequential damages arising directly or indirectly from any use of this material, which is provided "as is," and without warranties.

If you do not agree with these terms, return the book. Finally, use your head. Nothing in this book is intended to replace common sense.

Company and Group Partnership Opportunities

Custom Talks & Company-Specific Books

Please help me partner with organizations to share this information and help turn around as many families as possible. If you act now, you can be one of my key partners in teaching these skills.

I would be happy to coordinate with your company, school, association, church, or non-profit to print a customized Special Edition of this book. It will replace this page with highlights of your organization and its brand in each copy produced for your organization.

We can also partner concurrently with a charity of your choice. We would donate a part of the proceeds to it while benefiting your organization from the associated goodwill. This would get your brand in front of all of the charity's subscribers. I will prominently list key partners in my marketing materials, and our partnership can be featured in your marketing materials, demonstrating your concern for educating and equipping people with the skills to succeed in life.

There are many great ways you can offer your customers and clients extra value and make an impact with this book. You can give the customized book as a premium, as an added bonus with a purchase, with a mail-in coupon after a purchase, or as a free gift for making a phone call in response to a solicitation. You could give it to your customers as a free gift or at a reduced price with a purchase or contact to your organization.

Alternatively, you could give it to your team members for staff development. If you're in a financial advisor, banker, or relationship marketer-type role, you could give it to customers or clients. This way, you can develop multi-generational clients. Why not use the book to motivate your team in your down-line. Let's collaborate on creative ideas to share this information to benefit you and others!

I am also available to speak to your organization and participate in conferences. We could also develop break-out sessions or a tour to your branches to share these skills with all of your employees. In addition, I can help key partners design contests with challenges to departments, small groups, or individuals to see who can best apply the skills and gain the most net income. You can award prizes and incentives to further encourage them to implement this knowledge and teach others.

As you can see, there are countless ways to use this book to help grow and strengthen your organization. I have negotiated affordable volume pricing to dramatically reduce your cost per unit in order to fit your budget. Help your organization expand its exposure to a much larger audience and help adults learn crucial financial skills. Give me a call at 1-866-475-4675 or send me an e-mail at (jeff@lifescheatsheets.com) today to take advantage of this opportunity.

Free Gift

Forward this offer to your friends

As a way of saying thanks for your purchase, we are offering the free companion e-book, 11 Insanely Simple Ways To Slash Your Expenses Now! It started as a blog post that readers really liked.

With this simple e-book, you'll be able to quickly see many of the items that I outline in detail in the full book. You can give it to a friend, family member, coworker, or neighbor to let them see how to turn around their financial picture. If they want to learn more they can get the full book and companion workbook I have published. See Amazon for those.

To get free instant access, go to: FinancialReliefCoach.com

Chapter 1

Introduction

Are You Headed Toward A Financial Crisis?

"Most people think they have a money problem—what they really have is a decision problem."
"You're not trapped in debt—you're addicted to decisions that cause it."
"Your dream life is being siphoned away—one swipe at a time."
"Your spending is trading financial freedom for convenience."
"You are bleeding cash—become your Band-Aid to wealth."

<u>Have you ever thought?</u>
What if the power to change your financial life is already in your hands and you've chosen not to use it?
What if your real enemy isn't a lack of money, but autopilot spending?
What if freedom isn't found in more money, but in fewer

excuses?

How much longer will you let small pleasures steal big possibilities?

It's not the economy. It's not your boss. It's not even inflation. It's the daily decisions you're making without control and intention. They're draining your future, dollar by dollar, while you focus on the wrong things. Isn't it time to stop patching the symptoms and finally fix the real problem?

Reading can make you smart; the application of what you've read makes you wise and wealthy.

You've probably read and listened to lots of financial advice over the years. But how much have you looked into, decided is good advice, and then applied to your financial situation? If you're like most people, probably not much, but you still need help. We're going to change that now.

Picture this: you work hard every day and earn a decent income. But still, you feel like you're just scraping by. Sound familiar? If so, you're not alone. About 62% of Americans live paycheck to paycheck. This means that after paying bills, buying groceries, and covering basic needs, they have almost no money left. There is no safety net. No financial freedom.[1]

How is that possible? Because for most people, the problem isn't how much they make—it's how much they spend, often without realizing it. Did you know that the average American household throws away more than $7,000 each year on things they don't need? That's money lost on impulse buys, high convenience fees, unused subscriptions, and items that they don't need. Over a decade, that's $70,000 wasted. Think about how much it would be over a lifetime. We're talking about hundreds of thousands of dollars. This money could have built a financial cushion, paid off debt, or even helped you retire early.

Still not convinced? Let's break it down even further. The average middle-class person wastes $1,500 a year on unused memberships. This includes forgotten gym plans and streaming services hardly ever watched. Households throw away $1,800 worth of food annually due to waste and poor planning. The average American spends $3,000 a year eating out—often on meals they don't even remember enjoying. Credit card interest alone eats up $1,200 a year for the typical consumer.

Think about using half of that wasted money. You could pay off debt, build an emergency fund, or invest in your future. That's the difference between feeling constantly strapped for cash and getting ahead. The good news? You don't need to earn more money to change your financial future—you just need to use the money you already have wisely.

Common Cents: Stretch Every Dollar is a no-fluff, step-by-step guide to taking control of your financial life. This book won't tell you to live like a monk. You'll discover smart, proven ways to save money. You can keep more cash without giving up what you love. These techniques are for everyone. You don't need a degree to understand and apply them successfully. What you do need is a commitment to taking daily action to see the results you're looking for.

I created this list of solutions to help the struggling middle class. Using my years of turning around businesses and real estate projects, I have outlined some of the fastest ways to turn your financial life around.
I realize many people need to pinch their pennies to reach their own goals. All of these hints can be applied right away to start stretching your money. Taking 100% control of where every dollar goes is a crucial first step.

I refer to this process as the **Expense Assassin Strategy**—because you'll learn to eliminate waste with precision and purpose.

You'll learn how to manage your money through real-life examples and practical exercises.

Here's what you'll be able to do:

1. Track your spending and find hidden money leaks.
2. Cut costs on essentials while keeping your quality of life.
3. Negotiate better deals on purchases, bills, and services.
4. Slash grocery, dining, and transportation costs.
5. Reduce debt and grow savings with the money you save.

Your Big "WHYS"

To help you keep progressing, write down your biggest "whys" and several less important "whys." Consider why you want to cut expenses. Take a moment to note the feelings tied to your reason. Maybe you need to make a big purchase, maybe you're planning for retirement, or maybe you are overwhelmed by debt. Whatever your "whys" are, write them in clear detail. Read them and feel the associated feelings anytime you have a big hurdle, a bad day, or you're thinking of quitting.

Put a deadline on reaching each of your goals in this process. Make each of your goals aggressive. They need to challenge you and keep you moving forward with actions every day. You don't have to take big actions; just take a step or two every day. By the end of the week, you'll be impressed. By the end of the month, you'll be pumped up and ready to take bigger, bolder actions to move further. Build momentum by seeing little "wins" along the way. Stop to recognize and celebrate those wins. They will help build your confidence so you can step into any challenge.

Real Life Stuff

What I share here isn't theory—it has been tested in real life. You'll discover how to cut waste and not feel deprived. You'll also learn to stretch your dollars, so your hard-earned money works for you instead of slipping away. This book isn't just about saving a few bucks. It's about giving you lifelong control. Money stress is one of the biggest causes of anxiety in families today. Many people never learned the simple, practical strategies that truly make a difference. This book is about reducing financial stress and building a future where you feel secure.

One Last Hint

Some people find it easier to use my Common Cents workbook while going through this book. You can go to Amazon and purchase the workbook now if you want to complete the steps as you go. It's a companion tool that will walk you through all 11 Actions, completing the process in detail. Some like to do it at the end of the book while others like to do it as they go. It's your choice, but I wanted to make you aware of it as we get started.

<u>I'm betting one or more of these apply to you:</u>
Are you struggling to pay your monthly bills?
Are you preparing to buy a car or a home?
Do you need to find a way to pay for school?
Do you want to be debt-free?
Do you want to stop worrying about your money?
Are you ready to take control of your financial future?

Turn the page and get started!

SEIZE THE MOMENT,
JEFF "JJ" WILSON

Chapter 2

Action 1--Track Every Dollar You Spend

Need Accurate Baseline Data to Build Your Plan

Johnson Family's Financial Turnaround

The Johnson family thought they were doing everything right. They worked hard, paid their bills, and tried to save when they could. But every month, their bank account seemed to drain faster than expected. No matter how much they earned, they always felt like they were treading water financially. Debt kept piling up, and despite their best efforts, they had no idea where their money was going.

That changed when they made one simple decision: track every dollar for 90 days. At first, it felt tedious. Writing down every expense, no matter how small, forced them to face uncomfortable truths. They quickly realized their money was slipping through the cracks. Small, seemingly harmless expenses added up in ways they never imagined. Eating out, streaming services, subscription boxes, and impulse buys were costing them hundreds each month. What felt like minor indulgences were actually major drains on their finances.

Once they saw where their money was going, they made a plan. They started making intentional choices about their spending. The impact was immediate. With the money they saved, they began attacking their debt aggressively. Within two years, they had paid off $20,000 in loans and credit card balances. What seemed impossible became possible when they took charge of their spending.

Many families face money troubles, just like them. It's not that they earn too little; it's that they lack a clear view of where they are spending. This chapter will help you find hidden expenses, redirect your money, and take control of your future.[2]

The Hidden Cost of Not Tracking Your Money

According to a 2023 study by Intuit, a staggering 65% of Americans have no idea how much they spent last month. Not just on the little things—on everything. This lack of awareness has serious financial consequences. The study also found that households that actively track their expenses save 20-30% more annually compared to those who don't. That's thousands of dollars every year. You could use that money to build an emergency fund, pay off debt, or invest.[3]

Why does tracking have such a powerful effect? Because it forces accountability. It takes spending from something passive—where money just seems to "disappear"—to something intentional. When you see every transaction written down or logged in an app, you naturally become more mindful of your choices. That's the power of awareness—it allows you to take control of your money.

Many believe they have a solid grasp on their spending. But when they start tracking it, they see how much money is slipping away. That's why this chapter is so important. The first step to financial stability is seeing where your money is going. This practice is the start of building your financial plan you'll build in Action 2.

What Do Most People Do That Doesn't Work?

Most people rely on rough guesses, assuming they know their expenses. They glance at their bank app now and then, thinking it's enough. But memory plays tricks. That $5 coffee? Forgotten. The streaming service you never watch? Still billing you monthly. You'll end up with shortfalls which are deficits that will cause your financial plan to fall apart. These small leaks are easy to overlook, but they drain your finances drop by drop. Without a system, tracking expenses is like trying to fill a bucket with a hole in it. You end up wondering where your money disappeared.

What To Do Differently

Carry something with you at all times to jot down how much and on what you spent money. Keep a close eye on your spending. Write down every penny, especially cash purchases you might forget.

Writing down all your expenses lets you summarize them in your spreadsheet. This helps you track your spending for the month. There will be several smaller categories (subcategories) within an overall category. See examples of some of these that are typical in the chart in Action 2.

For example, you may have breakfasts, lunches, take-out meals, and suppers as subcategories of the meals category. It is helpful to break things down into little groups (subcategories) so you have a good handle on where you are specifically spending.

Track it daily. Set up your spreadsheet to keep running totals for each subcategory. Then, add these totals to get the category total for the month. Track all items for at least three months. Just like a business tracks every sale and expense, you need to know exactly what's coming in and going out. Tracking your finances helps you build a clear and complete plan. Then, you can stick to it, live within your means, and avoid overspending.

How To Start Tracking Income and Expenses

I suggest using a spreadsheet to track your expenses. If you don't have one, a lined notebook works too. Just write down your expenses by hand. Add a column for each of the following: Date, Category (as in the 2nd Action), Amount spent, and Description of the item. This will help you start tracking. It needs to be accurate more than fancy. See the example below.

If you use a debit/credit card, you can download the data to verify many of your purchases. Don't judge yourself, just track it daily. The more weeks and months you track, the better your plan becomes and the easier it is to be in control of your money.

DATE	CATEGORY/SUB	AMOUNT	DESCRIPTION

10 Steps to Tracking and Taking Control

1—Commit to Tracking Daily. The first step is deciding that you're all in. Tracking your spending only works if you do it consistently. Make a personal commitment to track every dollar for at least 90 days. If you miss a day, just get back on track as soon as possible. This habit will change the way you think.

2—Start Each Day Right. Tracking works best when it becomes routine. Each morning, check that you've recorded yesterday's expenses while they're still fresh in your mind. Set a daily alarm or reminder on your phone to track your expenses. This helps you stay consistent. Whenever you prefer, just have a set time each day to help you make tracking second nature.

3—Choose Your Method. There's no one-size-fits-all approach to tracking. Many people enjoy budgeting apps such as Mint or YNAB. These apps automatically categorize expenses and offer reports. I recommend and prefer spreadsheets where you can enter transactions manually and customize what and how you track. Some find that writing everything down in a simple notebook makes them feel more engaged in the process. The best method is the one you'll stick with. Experiment with different tools and find what works for you. The goal isn't perfection—it's consistency.

4—Record Every Transaction. Every dollar matters. Whether it's a paycheck, a refund, a gift, or cash from a side hustle, record every bit of income that comes in. Do the same for expenses—no matter how small. Log it all. Small expenses add up faster than you think, and the only way to see where your money is going is to track everything.

Honesty is key. If you're not truthful about your spending, you're only fooling yourself. Every purchase, even the ones you regret, needs to be recorded. Transparency helps you see where you might be overspending. It also lets you take control.

5—Keep Receipts. Small purchases slip through the cracks without receipts. Holding onto receipts gives you a foolproof way to record transactions accurately. A paper receipt or photo of it works to document it and get it in your tracking system.

6—Categorize Your Spending. Organize your expenses into clearly labeled categories. Break regular expenses into smaller groups (subcategories). For example, separate snack purchases from drive-thru meals. It makes it easier to identify areas where you might want to cut back.

Be focused when you establish your full list of categories and subcategories. Make certain that every expense you have fits naturally in a sub/category that is on your list. Put every expense of the same kind in the same sub/category. This way, you'll know your total is accurate for each type. It's ok to have a miscellaneous line item, but that should be for something that is a one-time, unusual cost.

7—Review Weekly. Set aside a day-time at the end of each week to go through what you've tracked. Look at how much you spent in each category. Are there any surprises? Did you overspend in one area? Did you forget about an expense? This review holds you accountable. It also stops small mistakes from becoming big financial issues. It also helps you stay motivated.

8—Identify Trends. After a month or two of tracking, patterns become clear. Maybe you're spending more on takeout than you realized. Maybe impulse buys are bigger than you thought. Identifying these trends allows you to make informed decisions. Instead of cutting back randomly, you can target the areas that are making the biggest impact on your budget.

9—Adjust Your Budget. After 30 days of real spending data, you can draft a budget that works for you. This step is part of building your overall financial picture budget in Action 2. Continue to update and modify this for a full 90 days to have a more accurate budget. Now you know how much you spend in each category and where adjustments need to be made. This puts you in control.

10—Celebrate Wins. Celebrate when you reach a milestone. Whether you cut spending, stick to your budget, or save more than planned, take a moment to enjoy it. Treat yourself to something small, but meaningful, as a reward. Acknowledging your success reinforces the habit and keeps you motivated.

Why Tracking Matters

Tracking your spending isn't about limits. It's about being aware, intentional, and in control. When you know where your money is going, you can make smarter choices for your financial future.

Awareness is Power--Most financial stress comes from uncertainty. Bills creep up, spending feels unpredictable, and financial surprises throw you off course. But when you track your spending, there are many fewer surprises. Awareness turns financial confusion into clarity.

Achieve Your Goals—Tracking your spending helps cut out costs that don't add value. This frees up cash for what truly matters. You might have great intentions to build an emergency fund, and then pay off debt, but without a system, those goals get pushed aside.

Build Discipline—Instead of swiping your card without thinking, you start asking yourself, Do I really need this? Is this worth it? With time, this awareness feels natural. It helps you build the discipline to manage your finances for the long haul.

Prepare for Emergencies—Life can be unpredictable. Cars break down. Medical bills appear. Unexpected costs often come at the worst times. Without an emergency fund, these moments can throw your entire budget off. A small sacrifice today can mean peace of mind in an emergency.

Ben Franklin's Ledger

Ben Franklin was a man of many talents—an inventor, a writer, a statesman—but one of his most powerful skills was his ability to track and manage his money. His wealth came from knowing exactly how to control the money he had to achieve financial freedom. He once wrote, "Beware of little expenses; a small leak will sink a great ship." He knew that careless spending, even if it's small, can hurt long-term financial success.

With many fewer resources, Ben became wealthy by taking control. What worked for Ben centuries ago still works today if you just take control.

Takeaways

1—Tracking your spending isn't just about numbers—it's about awareness. You begin to see your habits clearly. You recognize patterns, spot problem areas, and gain control over your finances.

2—Recording every dollar doesn't just show you where your money is going—it helps you find ways to save. Tracking exposes unnecessary costs, giving you the power to redirect your money toward things that truly matter.

3—Use an Excel-type spreadsheet so that you can electronically retain this information. Use its functions to combine spending into categories and manipulate the data to construct your budget.

4—Involve your entire family in this process. Get everyone working with you and helping with the process. This will make it easier and quicker to reach your goals.

5—Establish a full list of categories and subcategories. Make certain that every expense you have fits in a sub/category in your list and fits the respective category naturally.

Tracking is an initial key to gaining control of your finances. It may seem tedious, but it creates crucial baseline data needed to construct your complete financial picture in the next Action. Managing your money well takes work. With time, managing your money becomes less of a chore. It turns into a tool that empowers you. This helps you feel in control of your financial future and reduces stress. The more effort you put into tracking, the more financial freedom you'll gain in return.

Chapter 3

Action 2A--How to Construct Your Financial Plan

Restrict Distractions and Focus

CFO at 21 Years Old?

In the mid-80s, I became the CFO of a $12 million business. This included two companies: a public entity with 20 profit centers and a corporation with three plants and five divisions. I had just turned 21 years old so I had minimal experience running financial and IT departments or building detailed budgets. But I had already gotten the company out of a mess with the auditors, so I proved I could take on challenges. The President took a big chance on me. He gave me a "shot at the title," becoming CFO while I was still a kid studying for my business degree.

I went to work on building both entities' first detailed budgets on a new spreadsheet program. I built in all of the data to structure and fill them properly. I then learned to add look-up tables. This way, it could find the right classification and pay rate for each employee. It tracked years of experience and degrees and then filled in their pay rates for all 225+ staff.

It was very early for the use of spreadsheets and detailed budgets, but I taught myself and it all worked. I ultimately added the budgets to the financial statements for both entities. Then, I had it calculate variances for each line item in every profit center and division. If I can create detailed budgets that helped several businesses profit at 21, I know you can make a simpler one for your family. You're going to be confident and proud of yourself when we're done.

Americans Live Paycheck-to-Paycheck

As noted in the introduction, 62% of Americans live paycheck-to-paycheck. That means nearly two-thirds of all people are just one missed paycheck away from falling behind on their bills. They're working hard, bringing in a steady income, and yet struggling to stay afloat. Even more shocking? Almost 40% of those earning over $100,000 a year are also caught in this same cycle. It turns out that earning a six-figure salary doesn't guarantee peace of mind when it comes to money.

The common issue in these struggles is not low income. It's the absence of a clear financial plan that people can act on. Without a plan, even high earners can face lifestyle creep. This means they spend more just because they make more. Expenses rise silently until there's no cushion left. There's no safety net. No strategy. Just a monthly race to cover bills before the next paycheck hits. It's like treading water in the middle of the ocean—kicking as hard as you can, but getting nowhere.

This is exactly why building a financial plan matters. It's not about how much you make—it's about what you do with what you make. A detailed plan gives every dollar a purpose. It turns chaos into control. It replaces this paycheck mentality with confidence, clarity, and progress toward financial freedom.

Why This Chapter Matters

Many people believe they can manage their finances in their heads. But just like a business wouldn't operate without an accounting system, your household shouldn't either. A financial plan, or budget, is your guide to financial security. It's not a limit; it's a tool for gaining control.

What Most People Do

They "wing it," believing they can remember their expenses without tracking them. Most people assume they have a good grasp of their spending. They believe they can keep track of where their money goes just by thinking about it. They might know their rent or mortgage, car payment, and utilities. But after that, things get a bit unclear.

The problem? The human brain isn't designed to store and recall every financial detail. Life moves fast. Small expenses slip through the cracks. Receipts get tossed. By the time the month is over, they're left wondering why their bank account is lower than expected. Without tracking, it's impossible to know.

It's not intentional. People often underestimate their spending. They pay attention to big purchases but forget about the small ones that really add up. A $10 lunch here, a $20 impulse buy there, a $15 app subscription they forgot about—it all snowballs. By the end of the month, their estimate is miles off from reality, and they have no idea where the gap came from.

They fail to categorize spending accurately, leading to missing or forgotten expenses. They also don't get near specific enough because they are not tracking every item. Take groceries and dining out, for example. If someone budgets $600 for "food," they need to separate "groceries" from "restaurants." Otherwise, they won't know if they're spending wisely on groceries or overspending on takeout.

They create a plan based on partial information, leaving them short each month. What happens next? They scramble to cover the shortfall. They shift money from one category to another. They dip into their emergency fund, or worse, their credit card. Suddenly, they're playing financial whack-a-mole—moving money around just to stay afloat. By the time next month rolls around, the cycle starts all over again.

Why This Doesn't Work

A partial plan = an unreliable plan. If you forget expenses, you run out of money before the month ends. A financial plan is only as strong as its weakest link. Imagine a builder constructing a house but leaving out key measurements. The foundation is set, and the walls are built. But when it's time for the roof, they find they lack enough materials. The whole project falls apart. That's exactly what happens when items aren't fully accounted for in a financial plan.

This forces you to borrow from one category to cover another, leading to a financial snowball effect. When an unexpected expense pops up, they "borrow" from another category. Maybe they cut back on groceries to cover a surprise bill. Maybe they use their rent money to pay for car repairs, promising to make up for it later. But when "later" comes, they have another shortfall, and the cycle continues.

Instead of having a solid, predictable plan, everything becomes reactionary. It creates a cycle where you start the next month already in the hole. Without a complete, accurate plan, you are reacting instead of controlling your money. A financial plan should put you in the driver's seat. It should tell your money where to go before you even spend it.

9 Key Principles for an Effective Financial Plan

A financial plan is a strategy that helps you direct your money. The more intentional you are with your plan, the more financial stability and confidence you'll have. Most people let money control them instead of the other way around. A financial plan flips that dynamic. Every dollar should have a job—whether it's covering essentials, paying down debt, or saving for the future. It's your GPS for your money. If you don't map out where each dollar should go, you'll constantly wonder where your money went. Having a written plan ensures that your money is always working for you.

1--Choose the Right Tracking Method for You

Budgeting isn't complicated, but must be consistent. The best method is the one you'll actually use. Choose the App or spreadsheet you will use and start tracking. See the next chapter for further details on how to construct your plan.

2--The More Detailed, the Better

A vague budget leads to vague results. If you only track broad categories like "food" or "entertainment," you won't see where you're overspending. Instead, break your spending into detailed subcategories to pinpoint exactly where your money is going. The more specific your categories are, the easier it is to find problems and make smart changes. This will give you clarity.

3--Track Income/Expenses Before You Build Your Plan

A common mistake is building a budget based on what you think you spend, rather than what you actually spend. This leads to underestimating real expenses, which causes frustration and failure. Instead of guessing, track income/expenses diligently over at least 3 months while building your plan. Get at least 3 months of actual data before starting to rely on your financial plan. The longer you track your spending, the more accurate your budget will be. The key is to start with real numbers. You can't fix what you don't measure.

4--Have a Designated Budgeting Time

Set aside a consistent time each week to review your finances. Life gets busy. If you don't make budgeting a scheduled habit, it'll get pushed aside until your finances are in chaos. Think of it like a team meeting, but with yourself and your family. Review your spending and balances, then make any necessary adjustments. The goal is actively managing your money so you're in control. Choose a time when you're least likely to be distracted.

5--Adjust and Customize Over Time

Your first budget won't be perfect—and that's normal. The first few months will involve trial and error as you fine-tune your categories and spending estimates. Expect to make adjustments. You'll probably forget a few recurring expenses at first. You might realize some categories need to be split or combined. A rigid budget is doomed to fail. Life changes—your financial plan should too. As you refine your tracking, your plan will become more accurate and useful. View this as an evolving process. Adjusting your plan makes it more sustainable long term.

6--Prepare for Unexpected Expenses

Unexpected and irregular costs are only "unexpected" if you don't plan for them. For example, car repairs, medical bills, annual insurance premiums, and holiday gifts are all predictable estimates in the long run. To avoid financial shocks, set aside money every month for predictable, irregular expenses. Break these down into monthly contributions so you're not hit with a large bill all at once. Planning for them prevents last-minute financial stress. Adjustments should be made proactively rather than reactively. This prevents you from dipping into savings, racking up credit card debt, or scrambling to find extra cash when something pops up.

7-- Balance Between Fixed and Variable Expenses

Recognizing these differences helps prevent underbudgeting. Fixed expenses stay the same each month—rent, mortgage, car payments, insurance. Variable expenses change—groceries, gas, dining out, entertainment. The problem is that most people focus too much on their fixed costs and underestimate their variable ones. A financial plan must account for both. If your budget doesn't leave room for these variable swings in those areas, you'll constantly feel short on cash. Think of it like planning a road trip. Fixed expenses are your fuel and tolls while variable expenses are food, attractions, and unexpected detours. Your financial plan should be realistic about both types of costs so there are no nasty surprises.

8--Use Alerts for Due Dates

Automatic reminders prevent missed payments and late fees. Late fees and overdraft charges are some of the easiest ways to throw money away. They're completely avoidable. Setting up automatic reminders for bill due dates ensures you never miss a payment. Most banks and credit card companies offer text or email alerts. Budgeting apps can do the same. If digital tools aren't your thing, a simple calendar reminder works just as well. Think of it like setting an alarm for an important appointment. You wouldn't rely on memory alone to wake up for a big meeting. Your bills deserve the same level of attention. Automate where you can so you have less to remember.

9--Kaizen: Continuous Improvement for Your Finances

In Japanese business philosophy, "Kaizen" means continuous, small improvements that lead to big results over time. The same principle applies to your financial plan. Your first attempt at tracking expenses will feel messy. The key is to keep improving, little by little. Review your budget weekly. Adjust as needed. Identify wasteful spending. Find small changes that add up. Learn and adapt. Read about personal finance, listen to podcasts, and explore new ideas. With small, consistent improvements, you become more skilled and confident over time. The result? A financial plan that truly works for your life. People who succeed with money aren't always the smartest or the highest earners. They are the ones who stick to the process.

Takeaways

1—A financial plan is your roadmap. It gives you control over your money instead of leaving it to chance.

2—Winging it doesn't work. Forgetting and underestimating costs will always leave you scrambling.

3—By tracking income/expenses and continuously refining your plan, you build a strong financial future.

4—I suggest using a spreadsheet. This way, you can keep track of your information electronically. You can also use the spreadsheet functions to group spending into categories, find totals, and change data easily.

5—Include your whole family. This way, you can catch every bit of income and expense. It also helps everyone agree on the plan, so they'll support the goal.

6—Establish your sub/categories and make certain that every income/expense item fits in one of these categories naturally. This ensures every expense of the same kind gets put in the same category.

Some people hear "budget" and think of limitations. But a financial plan isn't about restriction—it's about freedom. It's about spending your money on what matters to you. Don't let it vanish in careless purchases. It's about prioritizing what matters. Once you shift your mindset, your plan is empowering. You use it as a tool to make better decisions.

Chapter 4

Action 2B--Draft Your Financial Plan

Take Action--Start Now

Start building your first financial plan now. This will keep it from feeling like a bigger challenge than it is. Getting your draft started now will allow you to revise and modify it as you gain more information and track more income and expenses.

A financial plan is only as good as the information that goes into it. The goal is to build a realistic, working financial strategy that helps you control all of your money. Follow these steps closely. They will help make your financial plan accurate, functional, and sustainable.

11 Steps to Your New Financial Plan

1—Gather All Past Spending Records—Most people think they know what they spend each month, but memory is unreliable. The only way to get an accurate picture of your financial habits is to look at your actual spending history. Start by gathering at least three months' worth of financial records that you've been tracking in Action 1. Include bank statements, credit card statements, debit card statements, cash receipts, and similar documents. Use these to check your tracking logs or spreadsheet from Action 1. The more data you have, the clearer your spending habits become. You want real numbers.

2--Choose the Right Tracking Method for You--Apps like Mint and YNAB help you track expenses automatically. They also sort your spending into categories. They can connect to your bank account and pull transactions in. However, some people find apps too restrictive. A custom spreadsheet can be a better option that gives you full control over your categories, formulas, and tracking methods. You can tailor it to fit your exact needs. You can find pre-made samples online or in Excel. Most of them can be modified to match your needs. Maybe a friend or coworker can help if you need it.

Track every penny using the techniques from Action 1. This helps you create a full picture instead of just relying on memory. There's no way around it. The key is consistency. Track as you go, not later when you've already forgotten things. If you want to get a handle on your finances, you have to track your spending. No exceptions. You must build your financial plan on reality, not estimates.

3—List Every Income Source—Income is just as important as your expenses in building this complete picture. Include all other income streams, beyond normal paycheck amounts.

• Include wages (net income after tax), bonuses, commissions, and side hustle earnings.

• Add investment income, child support, alimony, government benefits, and tax refunds.

• If your income varies, like for some in sales, use an average from the last year.

• If you work seasonally or on commission, use an average of your lower-earning months.

4—Categorize All Expenses—Expenses need to be organized so you can see where your money is going and identify areas for improvement. Start with bigger, broad categories, then break them down into subcategories. Some examples include:

A) Housing category:

• Rent/mortgage subcategory

• Property taxes subcategory

• Insurance subcategory

• Each utility subcategory

B) Transportation category:

• Car payment

• Gas

• Public transit

• Maintenance

• Repairs

• Insurance

• Plates/Registration

C) Food category:

• Groceries

• Breakfast

• Lunches out

• Dinners out

• Carry out

• Delivery

• Coffee shops

• Convenience buys

• Snacks

Do this for every income/expense item. They all must fit into a category. The more specific your breakdown is, the clearer your spending habits will become.

5—Include Every Expense--Cover all of the expenses in your plan even if they do not get paid every month. You will break down the expense into a monthly amount and put that money aside in your bank account. Then it will be there when you ultimately have to pay for it. For example, you usually pay property taxes every 6 months. However, each month, you'll set aside 1/6 of your total property tax cost in that expense subcategory. Then, at the end of the 6 months, you'll pay it from your cash account.

6—Identify Overlooked and Irregular Expenses—One of the biggest budgeting mistakes is forgetting about non-monthly expenses. These are the costs that don't appear on every statement but still impact your finances when they come due.

Check your past records for:

• Annual subscriptions

• Quarterly bills

• Car maintenance

• Medical costs

• Holiday and gift expenses

These costs are easy to forget until they hit. Instead of scrambling when they pop up, set aside money for them each month. When you plan for irregular expenses, very little catches you off guard.

7—Balance Between Fixed and Variable Expenses—Keep fixed expenses, like rent and insurance, apart from variable ones, like groceries and dining out. This helps you see how predictable your spending is. Fixed expenses are much more predictable. Variable expenses fluctuate, which means they need closer monitoring.

8—Maintain a "Miscellaneous" Category—Having a catch-all category prevents overspending elsewhere. No matter how well you plan, unexpected expenses will pop up. A last-minute gift. A school fundraiser. Without a buffer, those surprises can mess up your plan. A miscellaneous category is your financial shock absorber. It catches the random, unpredictable expenses so they don't force you to steal from other categories. A small percentage of your budget—maybe 1% can go here. If you don't use it, roll it into savings. A miscellaneous category gives your budget extra breathing room.

9—Compare Income vs. Expenses—This is when you see whether you're living within your means or overspending. Subtract total expenses from total income. What's the result? If income exceeds expenses: That's great! But don't let extra money sit idle. Assign it to something productive—build your emergency fund, pay off debt, then invest it for future growth. If expenses exceed income: You've got a problem. You're spending more than you earn. This causes more debt, stress, and financial instability. It's time for a turnaround, which is my strength. You must cut back ASAP and modify your budget or you risk foreclosure or bankruptcy, if it gets more out of control. First, cut variable expenses. Next, reduce fixed expenses. Focus on the biggest ones first. You've got to stop the financial bleeding or you are not going to make it.

10—Track and Refine—A budget isn't a one-and-done document. It's a living plan that evolves as your financial situation changes. At first, it changes every month, or even weekly, as you better understand each subcategory's total. The first version will be rough. The key is to track and refine it regularly. Review your financial plan weekly or in real-time to catch mistakes and adjust as needed. Make mid-month corrections if you overspend in one category—don't wait until the month's end. Watch for problem areas. If you often spend too much on dining out, change your habits or your budget. This step is like fine-tuning an instrument. Small adjustments improve performance. The more you track and refine, the stronger your financial plan becomes.

11—Commit to Using Your Financial Plan for 3 Months—Building a budget is a great start. Sticking to it is where the real challenge begins. Give your financial plan three months of consistent effort before making any major changes. The first month will feel messy. You'll forget expenses, make mistakes, and feel tempted to abandon the process. Push through it. By the second month, you'll start seeing patterns. You'll notice where your money leaks, where you can cut back, and where you might need to allocate more. By the third month, budgeting will feel like second nature. Tracking your spending won't seem like a chore—it'll be a habit. You'll feel in control of your money. The longer you stick with your financial plan, the more powerful it becomes. It's not about perfection. It's about progress.

Final Thoughts

Many people struggle with money. It's not always about low earnings. Often, it's about poor management of what they do have. Building your first financial plan takes effort, but the rewards are life-changing. Much less stress. Just clarity, control, and confidence in where your money is going.

Take Action Now! -- Build Your Draft Plan

Below is a sample of what a typical, simple Financial Plan could look like in a spreadsheet model. After making a basic plan, look for advanced tools. These can help you add formulas for totals, percentages, and comparisons to past months and years. You can also track variances. Feel free to adjust your plan so it's easy to use, understand, and helps with your decisions. This is your custom tool to help you control your resources so they work for you.

Set up income and expense sub/categories that match your specific situation like the examples in the chart below:

Fixed Items	Sub Category	**Variable Items**	Sub Category
House	Mortgage	House	Repairs
House	House Insurance	House	Utilities
House	Property Tax	House	Lawn
Cable/Internet		House	Snow Removal
Cell Phone		Groceries	
Savings	Emergency Fund	Eat Out	Restaurants
	Roth 401k	Eat Out	Snacks
	Roth IRA	Eat Out	Take out meals
	Excess to savings	Gas	
Debt	Student Loan	Medical Expenses	
	Monthly credit card	Clothing	
	Car payment	Travel	
Tuition		Personal Care	Haircut/Color
Netflix/Gaming			Chiropractor

You may want to set up your starting Financial Plan spreadsheet similar to the example below:

SIMPLE FINANCIAL PLAN SPREADSHEET in Excel--Doesn't have to be fancy or complicated								
Category	Sub-Category	Week 1	Week 1	Week 1	Week 2	Week 2	....	Monthly
		Budget	Actual	Net	Budget	Actual	(cont)	Totals
Income	Regular Pay	1000	1000	0	1000			
	Overtime	0	150	150	0			
	Side Gig	150	125	-25	150			
	Interest	25	30	5	25			
Expenses:								
Housing	Mortgage							
	House Insurance							
	Property Tax							
	Gas							
	Electric							
	Water/Sewer							
Eating Out	Restaurants							
	Lunches							
	Take-out							
	Snacks							
	Convenience							
	Delivered							
	Coffee Shops							
Vehicles	Car payment 1							
	Car payment 2							
	Insurance							
	Plates							
	Gas							
	Maintenance							
	Repairs							
	Public Transp							
Savings	Emergency Fund							
	Roth 401k							
	Roth IRA							
	Excess Savings							
Medical	Insurance							
	Co-pays							
	Deductible							
	Co-insurance							
	Surgery loan pmt							
Online	Internet							
	Cable							
	Netflix							

This is only a partial spreadsheet to show you the structure and how I would build it to work for you each week of the whole month. You would have to add the columns for the extra weeks in the month and build in formulas for the monthly totals. Keep each month separate. Don't override the prior month with the new one. In Excel, you can set up a tab for each month of the year and copy the spreadsheet month by month. You will continue to modify it as you catch new items and other things that needs to be revised. Make it how it works best for you. They key is to use it regularly.

Chapter 5

Action 3--Negotiate Purchases and Use More Cash

Practice This Skill Daily

Negotiate With Walmart—No Way?

It was a few days after Christmas and Walmart had all of the Christmas stuff heavily marked down. We have a vaulted great room with a 17' ceiling and we saw 14' pre-lit Christmas trees marked 50% off of $450. There were six of them. Most people couldn't use them with their height so I had leverage right away. I always need to find leverage when I am going to negotiate. My wife, Beth, was with me, and we would like one of these huge trees. I had gotten us deals on 5 other typical trees over the years with storage foreclosure auctions and wholesale deals. So, we didn't need any more trees. I said I'm not paying over $50 for any tree. I knew someone else with a vaulted room. I called them, and they wanted one too if I could get a great deal. This gave me more leverage. I would now buy two and take them with me (so no shipping coordination—more leverage) if I got my price.

Beth is an experienced attorney who negotiates as part of her role. She said there is no way they will sell those for $50 since they are already 1/2 price at $225, so you might as well not even try. I love a great challenge and I had nothing to lose. I didn't have the tree and didn't need it. It was a "want," so my Best Alternative To a Negotiated Agreement (BATNA) was to walk away. They would keep them for the next year in up stock, which costs them money tied up in inventory (more leverage). They are in the business of inventory turnover as quickly as possible.

I talked with the clerk at the display, and she turned me down. She said they were marked down as far as they would. I politely asked who the manager of the department was, what her name was, and where she was. She took me to her. I explained all of the leverage points I mentioned above in a logical fashion, and she barely hesitated. She said, "Let me go get a change order form, and I'll write it up. You can take it to the cashier, pay, and pull around to pick them up." And yes, for $50 each. Beth's mouth fell open because she didn't believe what had just happened. Jeff for the win. The next issue was that they were over 100 pounds each and in huge boxes, so we could only take one home at a time. But it all worked out.

A month later, I decided to do the same thing at the same Walmart with a digital camcorder. I researched online and found some refurbished items that were like new returns. I went back to the manager and presented my case with leverage points. Then, Walmart matched the price with a new change order. I walked out with a new camcorder, and Beth decided to just watch rather than give an opinion this time. The point is that you can negotiate with almost anyone. Just do a little planning before you talk with them. Have your leverage points laid out, as well as your BATNA, and rehearse your case a bit in your mind before presenting it. Always be polite. Try to get them to like you and be on your side. Each manager has an approval level, so you may need to go up the chain to achieve your goal.

Give It a Try—You Can't Lose Something You Don't Have

Most people assume negotiating is awkward, pointless, or even embarrassing. Studies suggest that only 28% of Americans have ever attempted to negotiate a purchase—yet, of those who did, a staggering 89% successfully got a better deal. That means the vast majority of people who ask for a discount actually save money—yet most never even try. Why? Because they assume prices are fixed, they fear rejection, or they simply don't know how to ask.

At the same time, research on spending habits reveals another surprising truth: people spend up to 83% more when paying with credit cards instead of cash. Swiping a card feels effortless, almost like spending Monopoly money. But, handing over physical cash creates a much stronger sense of financial loss. The result? More impulsive purchases and bigger totals. Businesses know this psychology. That's why they promote card payments and avoid mentioning that prices can be negotiated.[4]

If negotiating works well and using cash helps cut spending, why don't more people do it? The answer lies in habit, mindset, and knowledge. This chapter will help you overcome fear, boost your negotiation skills, and use cash to gain full control of your finances.

The Psychology of Why Most People Overpay and Overspend

Most people never even think to question the price of something. They see a number on a price tag or a bill and assume that's it. Negotiating feels uncomfortable, like something pushy salespeople or extreme bargain hunters do. It's easier to just pay what's asked than risk an awkward conversation. Many people also fear rejection—what if the cashier or clerk laughs at them? What if they look cheap? Businesses price their services with good margins, hoping most people won't push back.

At the same time, credit cards have completely changed the way people spend. There's no physical exchange, no moment of pause. It's just a swipe. I'll deal with it later. But those swipes add up fast. Studies show that people consistently spend more and buy more frequently when using credit cards. Retailers like plastic because it makes you less aware of your spending. You end up buying more.

Credit cards used irresponsibly create an invisible financial leak that drains your money. It's easy to think the problem is just high interest rates, but the bigger issue is psychological. You don't notice the loss right away. When the bill arrives weeks later, it's tough to link the spending to exact purchases.

8 Strategies for Negotiating and Using Cash More

The way you spend and manage money has more power over your financial future. Remember, every salary talk, purchase, and bill can help you earn or save money. You control how much.

1—Most Businesses Are Prepared to Negotiate

Many businesses don't expect everyone to pay full price. They set their prices knowing that some people will ask for a better deal. For example, mechanics often change their prices. They do this based on competitors' offers and customer requests. Comparison shopping isn't only about getting the best deal. It's also about using competition to your advantage. If one company won't budge on price, chances are their competitor might. Having multiple quotes puts you in the driver's seat. Let businesses know you're shopping around, and they'll often lower their price.

2—Companies Often Reward Customers Who Ask

Many companies offer unpublished discounts for customers who ask. They don't promote these deals because they don't want to lower prices for everyone. But if you call and mention a competitor's rate or say you're considering canceling, they often have a retention offer ready. They'd rather keep you as a customer at a lower rate than lose you altogether. If you never ask, you'll never know what discounts are available. The worst that can happen is they say "no." The best that can happen? You lower your bill for months or even years.

3—Make Negotiation a New Skill

Negotiation doesn't have to be complicated. Sometimes, all it takes is one simple question. Asking, "Is that the best you can do?" forces the other person to consider whether they have room to adjust. They may not offer a lower price outright, but they might throw in a bonus, waive a fee, or find a better deal.

For example, we used to own a timeshare. I knew each place we traded our week for wanted us to consider buying their timeshare. I used to negotiate very good incentives just to listen to their pitch for two hours. They once gave us four, 18-hole rounds of golf with a cart. This was on a professional course that would have cost more than $200 per round. Is $800+ worth two hours of vacation time?

Like any skill, negotiation gets easier the more you do it. Start with low-pressure situations where the stakes are small. Ask for a discount at a flea market or ask to waive a fee at a hotel. These small wins build confidence. The more you practice asking, the easier it gets to negotiate bigger things. This includes your salary, rent, or buying a house.

Rejection feels personal, but in negotiation, it's just part of the process. No one is going to laugh at you, blacklist you, or take away what you already have. But if you never ask, you guarantee that you'll keep overpaying. Most people expect pushback in negotiations. Many are ready to offer something better if you show confidence. The only way to find out is to ask.

Most people hate awkward silence. Salespeople and service representatives are no exception. After making an offer, resist the urge to fill the gap. Stay quiet and let them respond. That pause puts subtle pressure on them to consider your request rather than dismiss it. Many times, they'll offer something just to break the silence.

4—Several Small Wins Add Up Over Time

Saving 5% on one bill might not seem like a game changer. But multiply that across all your monthly expenses and the impact becomes massive. A small discount today turns into hundreds or even thousands of dollars saved over a year. That's money you can put toward something meaningful. The key is consistency. Small wins create serious financial momentum and confidence.

Don't let your bills auto-renew at the same (or higher) rates without question. At least once a year, take some time to call competing providers for each expense you have. Adopting the mindset that every price is flexible shifts how you approach spending. You start questioning, researching, and looking for ways to get more for less. Ask if they have any promotions, discounts, or loyalty rewards, then do the same with your current provider. If they won't budge, mention that you're shopping around. Many companies have retention departments whose job is to keep customers by offering better deals. A few phone calls could save you hundreds of dollars. I've done this and saved $1,500 on annual property taxes and $1,800 on annual insurance, to name a couple.

5—Cash Spending Can Cause Pain; Just Pause

When you use cash, you feel every dollar leaving your hands. Psychologists call this "paying pain"—the discomfort you feel when parting with your money. The more you feel it, the more careful you are when you spend. To cut spending naturally, try using cash for daily purchases.

It's easy to overspend when all you have to do is swipe a card. Cash forces discipline. Withdraw a set amount each week for your discretionary spending—groceries, entertainment, dining out—and once it's gone, it's gone. Physically seeing the money dwindle makes you more mindful of each purchase. You'll naturally start prioritizing what truly matters and cutting out the extras.

Wait. If something isn't essential, don't buy it immediately. Impulse spending is the enemy. If your credit or debit card isn't with you, you can't mindlessly buy something. Buying when you're excited, stressed, or frustrated rarely ends well. Emotions cloud judgment and make it easier to justify unnecessary purchases. Walk away, sleep on it, and see if you still want it the next day. Most of the time, the initial excitement fades, and you realize you don't need it.

6—Avoiding Credit Cards Reduces Overspending

Research shows that shoppers who pay with cash feel more emotionally attached to their purchases than those who use credit cards. These shoppers also thought about what they would lose by not being able to spend that money on something else. Psychologists tested this idea by selling university logo mugs at a discount. Then, they asked participants how much they would sell their mug back for. Cash buyers wanted 35% more than their purchase price. Credit card users wanted only 80% of what they paid.

Paying cash may also save you money. Every time you use a credit card, the business pays a processing fee—usually between 2%-4% of the total sale. Many companies would rather not pay that money to the credit card companies. If you offer to pay with cash, check, or even direct bank transfer, they may be willing to pass the savings on to you. Many gas stations offer a lower price for cash transactions.

7—Negotiating Your Salary/Side Income is Just as Important

Saving money is one side of the equation. Earning is the other. Many people underprice themselves. They think their boss won't give them a raise. Or, they accept whatever a client offers for freelance work. But just like expenses, wages/rates are often flexible. If you never ask for a raise, you might be leaving thousands of dollars on the table. A raise compounds over time. When you earn more, your financial progress accelerates. Negotiating your income requires asking the question.

8—Negotiation Works—Make It a Habit

Every time you successfully negotiate a lower price, a waived fee, or a better deal, write it down. Keeping a log of your savings isn't just a confidence booster—it's proof that negotiation works. Over time, you'll start seeing patterns. You'll discover where you negotiate best and which businesses are flexible. You'll also see how much money you've saved just by asking.

Each small win reinforces your ability to advocate for yourself. If they accept your first offer, you realize it might have been too high. Next time, you should start with a lower offer. I'm naturally competitive, so I turn it into a game. I see how aggressive I can be while still getting reductions. The confidence you gain spills over into other areas of your life.

Negotiation keeps more money in your pocket right now. You can save money right away. For example, you might knock $20 off your internet bill or get a lower rate on car insurance. There's no waiting for compound interest or market fluctuations. Every dollar you don't spend is a dollar you can put to use elsewhere.

Negotiating and using cash aren't just strategies—they're habits that put you back in control of your finances. Every time you choose cash over plastic, you're making a conscious decision about your spending. These small shifts create long-term financial results.

Exercise—Start Right Now!

1--List 3 Purchases or Bills You Will Negotiate This Week

Write down three expenses you regularly pay that might have room for negotiation. Jot down how much you're currently paying. Then add some leverage points to try to convince the party to reduce your bill. Decide if you will ask for a discount, promotional rate, extra service at no cost, etc. Have competitor's prices available. Have a plan and practice your delivery before approaching the vendor.

2--Withdraw a Set Amount of Cash for the Week

Decide how much you'll need for everyday purchases and withdraw that amount in cash. Only use this cash for specific expenses you have decided. As the week goes on, track how your spending changes. Do you hesitate before making a purchase? Are you more aware of how much you're spending? Many people naturally spend less when using cash because they see the money leaving their hands. Pay attention to how it affects your habits.

3--Attempt a Simple Negotiation

The next time you buy something, try negotiating to get a lower price, waive a fee, or get more goods/services for the same price. Ask a store if they will price match a competitor. The goal is to build the habit of asking.

4--Compare a Card Purchase vs. a Cash Purchase

Pick a small but necessary item. Buy it once with a credit/debit card and take note of how it feels. Then, later in the week, buy the same item with cash. Did you hesitate more with the cash purchase? Did you feel the spending more? Were you tempted to add extra items when using your card? Reflect on the differences and consider how using cash more could change your financial habits.

5--Reflect on Your Results

At the end of the week, take a few minutes to evaluate what happened. Were you able to negotiate a discount on any of your bills? How much did you save? What could you do differently next time to save more? Did using cash help you avoid unnecessary purchases? Did you feel more in control of your money? Consider what you learned and how you can apply it going forward. If something worked well, make it a new habit.

Takeaways:

1--Attempt to negotiate more income and better pricing on every income stream, expense, debt, and investment. You can only gain.

2--Always know your leverage points and BATNA. Practice your proposal in your head before the negotiation.

3--Don't talk yourself into NOT negotiating. Shut down the voice in your head and take action. Force yourself to negotiate purchases you never have before. It helps you control the fear in your mind, builds your confidence, and makes it a habit.

4--Use cash for expenses more often because it reduces your spending frequency and amounts.

5--Be very careful using credit/debit cards because you spend more easily and usage can get out of hand.

The money that you've earned through negotiation is a tax-free raise. The wealthiest people in the world rarely pay full price.

Chapter 6

Action 4--Minimize Eating Out

Fully Controllable Variable Cost

NOTE: Once you complete the first 3 Actions, you can complete Actions 4-11 in any order. Customize the order to your specific needs so you can get as much benefit out of each one as quickly as possible.

I'm Outta Here

Last year on my birthday, we went to a nice restaurant. My wife likes to splurge occasionally. I don't value food at all, so I cannot stand to pay much for food. We went to this more expensive local Italian place that is family-owned. Knowing we had been there in the past, it was about $20 per entrée plus tax and tip, so we were going to spend about $25 a person. On your birthday, you get your meal free, which meant we would spend about $25. We sat down and checked the menu. The $20 entrée had jumped to $40. So, a piece of lasagna, a small side, and a glass of ice water would cost about $50 with tax and tip, just for my wife. I looked at her and said, "That's not even close to worth it." She agreed. We politely told the waitress we needed to meet someone else (excuse). Then, we got up and left.

You've got to have the guts to walk if somebody's trying to gouge you, and that is what I felt was happening. I've never been back. There are so many places to eat here that I have no problem finding those that are reasonable. Some couples I know go there and spend $125-$150 because they get an alcoholic drink and dessert. I can get a full lasagna that will take us the entire week to eat for multiple meals for $18 at Gordon's Food near me. There's no way I'm paying $50 at any restaurant for one piece. It's never going to be worth it to me.

You need to assess the value of what you're going to be asked to pay. Then, decide if it's worth it, no matter if you can afford it or not. In this case, there was no way it was worth it to me, so I said I'm outta here. I'm very glad I did, and I would do it again. It boosts your confidence. You take charge of your future instead of feeling pressured to overspend.

Why This Chapter Matters

Eating out is one of the easiest ways to lose control of your spending. It doesn't hit all at once like a big purchase. It seeps into your budget in small, forgettable transactions. Meals out can add up quickly, quietly taking hundreds or even thousands from your account each month. You don't even feel it until your bank balance is lower than expected, and you have no idea where all your money went.

Unlike your mortgage or car payment, restaurant spending isn't set in stone. It's one of the most flexible parts of your budget, which means it's also one of the easiest places to rein in costs. It's a variable cost, which means you have complete control. Cutting back doesn't mean giving up dining out entirely. It means being intentional. Decide when and where to eat out. Order wisely. Make sure each dollar you spend supports your financial goals.

What Most People Do

Most people don't think twice about how much they spend at restaurants. Eating out feels normal. It's social, it's convenient, and it's fun. You don't sit down and calculate how those dinners, takeout, and drinks are adding up. Before you know it, a harmless habit becomes a financial drain.

People often spend more than they should simply because they're with friends or family. Many don't want to skip the appetizer or drink water. And when the bill comes, it's easy to just split it equally, even if your meal was half the price of the others. Some even pick up the check without thinking.

What's worse, many of these same people are struggling financially. They're living paycheck to paycheck. They have credit card debt they're barely keeping up with. Some are facing foreclosure. Yet they continue spending at restaurants as if none of that is happening. By the time they check their credit card bill, the damage is done.

Why This Approach Fails

A big part of your paycheck now goes to restaurants. This leaves you struggling to pay other bills. It's easy to assume you're spending "about the same," but it can fluctuate wildly. When this area is too high, something else in your budget has to give. If you're putting dining expenses on a credit card and not paying it off immediately, the cost is even worse. You're literally financing meals out. Months later, you're still paying off a burger and fries you charged.

Restaurant prices have jumped 40-50% since the pandemic. Still, most people haven't changed their habits. The cost of eating out is higher than ever, but many still dine out as if nothing has changed. They justify the expense because "everyone else is doing it." They might look like they have it all together, but behind the scenes, they're drowning in debt.

9 Key Strategies to Reduce Restaurant Spending

1—Understand the True Cost of a Restaurant Meal

A menu price is just the starting point. Many people look at a meal's price and think that's all they pay. But restaurant bills often have hidden costs that can add up quickly. Tax and tip alone can add 20-30% to your total, and that's before considering upsells like extra toppings, drinks, or sides. Take a simple $12 meal. Add a drink for $3, tax for another $1, and a 20% tip—suddenly, it's now close to $20. That's almost double the original price. Multiply that across several meals a month, and the difference is staggering. Before ordering, take a second to run the numbers. Become aware before overspending.

2—Don't Let Other People's Spending Dictate Yours

It's easy to get caught up in the moment when dining out with friends. Multiple people order appetizers, get cocktails, and add dessert. You don't want to be the odd one out, so you do the same—ignoring the fact that your budget says otherwise. Rarely is anyone paying attention. You don't need to match their appetizers or cocktails. Order what your budget allows and enjoy being out. It's none of their business.

3—Avoid "Little Extras" That Inflate the Bill

Many restaurant bills don't balloon because of the main entrée—they do because of everything added on top. Drinks, appetizers, and desserts double or even triple what you thought you were going to spend. Many people don't realize how much money they throw away on overpriced beverages. Alcohol is the worst. Restaurants thrive on high-margin drink sales. Also, don't order a la carte. Adding the items together is usually more than an entrée. Stick to water, skip the extras, and watch your bill shrink. Water is free, healthier, and eliminates one of the restaurant's highest markup items.

In my MBA, I did a study on Pepsi vs. Coke products. I set up a taste test booth on campus. I found restaurants spent a nickel ($0.05) on each glass of pop, and they were charging $1.50 at the time, and now it's $2.50-3.00.

Restaurants often upsell by suggesting extras. They don't always mention the extra costs for items like cheese, tomatoes, or dipping sauces. So to avoid surprises, ask if there's an extra charge. Then, decide if you want to pay more for these extras.

We are purposely careful with our spending when we go out. We also don't drink, so we spend much less than many of our friends. For example, we go to a fun steak place, share a meal and our entire bill is about $20. As you can see, you can still go out, but just be choosy about what you spend on.

4—Be Selective About Where You Eat

Not all restaurants have the same prices. Choosing the wrong one can really cost you. A lot of people make the mistake of sitting down at a restaurant before checking the prices. By that point, it feels awkward to leave, so they stay—spending way more than they intended. The solution is simple: do your research before you go. Check the menu online, look at the pricing, and decide if it fits your budget. If it's too expensive, don't be afraid to walk away. Re-read my introductory story. You're not obligated to stay.

When you eat at a restaurant, remember this: you're not just paying for food. You also cover rent, labor, utilities, and profit. That's why a simple pasta dish that costs $3 to make at home can cost $18 at a restaurant. Cooking at home slashes these unnecessary costs. A $50 restaurant meal could turn into four homemade dinners for the same price. Many restaurant meals contain hidden sugar, salt, and fat, making them far less healthy. At home, you decide the portion sizes, the quality of ingredients, and the nutritional value.

5—Use Smart Discounting Strategies

There's zero reason to pay full price when so many discounts are available. These deals can easily cut your bill by 30-50% if you take a few extra minutes to find them. Saving money is smart, but many people don't take advantage of the many discounts for dining out. Many restaurants have BOGO (Buy-One-Get-One) deals, Groupon discounts, and loyalty rewards. These can lower your costs. Spending a few extra minutes to find a deal before dining out can save you money. You might pay $40 for a meal, but with a little effort, you could get the same meal for just $20.

Happy hours, early birds, weekly promotions, and birthday rewards can add discounts to your meal. If you're going to eat out, why not get the best deal possible? We like to use Entertainment and Save Around restaurant coupon books. Many of the options in these are Buy-One-Get-One deals, and the books on sale can cost $15 for the year, plus you can get one or more free if you buy multiples. Last year we had three of each and spent about $45 on them, yet I quickly calculated at the end of the year we had saved over $1,000.

6—Learn Portion Control

Most restaurants serve portions that are far bigger than what one person needs or wants. Instead of ordering a full-sized meal, consider splitting an entrée with a partner. It's usually more than enough food, and you instantly cut your cost in half. If sharing isn't an option, make leftovers part of your strategy. Before you start eating, mentally divide your meal in half. Eat one portion at the restaurant and take the rest home for another meal. You double the value of what you paid for, turning one restaurant visit into two meals instead of one. Another great hack is to order an appetizer as your main course. Many appetizers are just as filling as a regular meal but cost less. Some restaurants even let you order a lunch-sized portion of a dinner entrée at a lower price. It also helps you avoid overeating.

7—Compare Restaurant Spending to Long-Term Value

A $75 meal might not seem like a big deal at the moment, but step back and think about what else you could do with that money. That same $75 could cover a full tank of gas or a new pair of running shoes. Over time, these decisions add up to real financial progress. A $75 dinner lasts an hour while a $75 investment lasts far longer. If you had to choose, which would you rather have? The money you save from cutting back is redirected to something better. Ask yourself: Is this restaurant meal worth what I'm giving up? I like Invicta watches. I can get a nice one for $100-150 that will last me 20 years, and I'll use it regularly. Compare that one-hour meal to 20 years. It is no comparison. I don't value food at all, so it is a very easy decision for me. Which feels like the better move to you?

8—Use Cash Instead of Cards

Swiping a card makes spending too easy. You don't feel the impact of your money leaving, which leads to ordering without restraint. Credit cards can trap you in a risky spending cycle. If you don't pay off the full balance each month, you end up paying interest on meals you've already eaten. Paying with cash creates a natural spending limit. When you only bring a set amount to cover your meal, you can't overspend.

9—Set a Monthly Maximum

Decide in advance how much you're willing to spend on dining out each month. Without a clear limit, it's easy to let restaurant spending spiral out of control. Setting a firm number ensures you stay in control. Pick a number that fits within your overall financial plan. If you've been spending $500 a month on restaurants, challenge yourself to cut that in half. Stick to it like it's a hard rule. Track each dining expense as you go so you know exactly where you stand. Every dollar spent on dining out is a dollar lost (sunk cost). It could have worked for you elsewhere instead. That's opportunity cost. That $100 dinner? It could have gone toward an extra credit card payment, a stock investment, or savings for a future home. Discipline here means more money for what matters.

Practical Exercise: The Restaurant Savings Experiment

This step-by-step challenge is designed to open your eyes to how much you're spending on restaurants. It shows how much you can save by making small, intentional changes.

1—Review Your Dining Out Expenses

Pull your last three months of bank statements and credit/debit card transactions. Write down every single restaurant visit, takeout order, and bar tab. No skipping any payments. Total it up. Most people are shocked when this number is in the hundreds or thousands of dollars. Now ask yourself: Would I make the same choices again if I had that cash back in my pocket?

2—Set a New Monthly Dining Budget

Now that you know the actual number, it's time to cut that hard. Challenge yourself to reduce it by at least 50% for the next month. This might seem drastic, but remember, this is a fully controllable expense—it's not a necessity. Decide and write it down. This is your limit, period. That means checking your balance before making plans and saying no when a meal doesn't fit the budget.

3—Identify Three Ways to Cut Costs

Pick at least three cost-saving strategies to implement this month.

Here are some easy ways to save money:

• Drink water.

• Skip appetizers.

- Use restaurant coupons.
- Look for BOGO deals.
- Find discounts.
- Choose budget-friendly spots.
- Order an appetizer as a meal.
- Share a full entrée.
- Check menu prices before you go out.

Choose your strategies now and stick to them.

4—Test a More Frugal Dining Out Strategy

When the bill comes, take a moment to compare what you spent to what you normally would have spent. Did you feel deprived? Did you still enjoy the experience? Most people find that making adjustments barely affects their dining experience. It's about retraining yourself to be more mindful.

5—Compare Savings at Month-End

After 30 days, total up what you spent on dining out this month and compare it to what you were spending before. How much did you save? Now, decide where that extra money is going. Make it count. Assign it to something meaningful. Put it toward an emergency fund, pay off a chunk of debt, or invest it. Once you see how easy it is to cut back without feeling deprived, it's much easier to keep that momentum going.

Takeaways

1—Monitor your spending in real-time. Only spend what fits your budget. Only pay for what you have agreed to pay for. If there is an error, don't be afraid to nicely disagree with the bill and ask for it to be changed. Be firm. They have a lot of competition you can go to.

2—Don't feel pressured to match others' spending habits.

3—Question whether the cost is worth it. If the prices seem unreasonable, walk away.

4—Be careful—restaurant prices surged during the pandemic. Many places never lowered their prices back down. Many restaurants have chosen to add premium pricing to everything, some 40-50%. Now that those materials are available at lower prices, they never reduced the prices.

5—Eating at home is almost always the cheaper option. This is one of the easiest places to save.

This chapter focuses on smart decision-making. Every dollar you spend at a restaurant is a dollar that could be working for you somewhere else. The question isn't whether you can afford to eat out. It's whether you can afford to let it hold you back. Shifting your mindset from "This is just what eating out costs" to "I decide what I'm comfortable spending" is one of the most empowering financial moves you can make.

Chapter 7

Action 5--Use A Grocery List

Simple Yet Powerful

Cash Flow Nightmare

I led a financial turnaround a few years ago at a large, $55MM non-profit entity with 15+ sites. They had taken on new enterprise healthcare software that didn't work well. They were owed 5X (500%) their usual amount. This was due, in large part, to over 100,000 Medicaid invoices being rejected. Cash flow was terrible. They were operating on loans because so many bills were rejected due to software problems.

I evaluated staff skills for those who could spend part of their day assessing errors and fixing invoices online in real time. As soon as we began, I started a list of error codes. For example, when we found Error 22, we figured it out and wrote down the steps to fix it. Then, I teamed up with the software developers to patch the issue. We kept adding errors and the related correction to the list which grew as we found more and more issues. We accumulated several pages of corrections by error number. This made it easy to find the code and fix it quickly.

This list became the "bible" for staff correcting errors. It let them easily find their error and correct as many as they could each day. We improved our speed and finished fixing the errors months later. We collected millions of dollars. We cut the inflated A/R Aging total by 90%. This dropped what was owed to the company to half of what it was before the new software. A huge cash flow improvement.

Your grocery list can cut your spending and increase cash flow, too. It helps you stay focused. It lets you shop faster, stick to your budget, and get in and out of the store quickly.

What Most People Do that Doesn't Work

Many people go grocery shopping without much planning. They hope to come up with a meal plan on the spot. They enter the store unsure of what they need. Instead, they let the shelves choose for them. This results in picking up anything that looks appealing at the moment. Impulse buys quickly add up, driving the total bill far beyond what was budgeted.

Shoppers frequently forget vital items that they intend to purchase. Now they're forced to make an additional trip back to the store, adding even more to the total cost. How often have you stood at the register, eyes wide as the cashier rings up way more than you expected? This lack of preparation rarely works in your favor. Not having a list can cause you to overspend, waste time, and miss opportunities. Are you ready to break this cycle and take control?

What To Do Differently That Works

Preparation equals control. Planning ahead helps you control your spending. It also lets you make smart choices at the grocery store. A well-crafted grocery list is your roadmap. It directs you toward the items you truly need while keeping distractions at bay. When you enter the store with a clear list, you know what to pick up and what to ignore. This focus minimizes distractions. A detailed grocery list ensures that you never overlook the items you truly need. Writing down everything important helps you remember key items. This way, you can avoid costly return trips that waste your time.

Before you set foot in the store each week, take a few moments to review paper and online sale ads. Also, browse your favorite store's websites or mobile apps. Set a reminder on your phone or mark it on your calendar to make this a consistent habit. These show discounted items and special deals you can add to your plan. This transforms routine shopping into a strategic money-saving opportunity.

Coupons are money-saving tools. Each coupon you use is a small victory that adds up to significant savings over time. Think about the benefits of choosing store brands and buying in bulk at wholesale clubs. Store brands usually offer the same quality as name brands but cost less. Buying in bulk can save you money over time, often making up for the small fee of a wholesale club membership. Wholesale clubs offer cheaper gas prices, too.

I learned about the massive power of coupons a number of years ago when I watched an extreme couponers show. Joni Meyer-Carothers, a local contestant to me, almost won the entire competition. She and the others did unbelievably well. I saw them buy around $4000+ worth of groceries in one setting using a huge amount of different types of coupons. They left with multiple carts full of groceries, paying just a few dollars. All of the best ones paid nearly nothing.

They have a system you would have to follow closely, pulling coupons from several places. You would also have to be very organized with a great filing system. Joanie's efforts allowed her to give away 80+% of what she bought to people in need, pantries, and other causes. I've talked with her and am impressed with her and the concept. TLC helped her publish an Extreme Couponing book that is worth every penny. You could earn back the $15 for that book several times over on your first shopping trip. You don't have to go to the extremes that Joanie and the other contestants did. You can still save a lot by using some of her methods.

Each planned shopping trip reinforces your commitment to your budget and long-term goals. Each step can change your grocery shopping into a smart, money-saving habit. By planning ahead and sticking to your list, you not only save money but also take control of your financial future.

Exercise--Mastering the Grocery Experience

1—Set Aside Time

Begin by choosing a quiet, uninterrupted 30-minute window before your next grocery trip. Focus solely on mapping out your shopping strategy.

2—Research

Dive into your local store's website or mobile app to explore the weekly sale ads. Gather the latest deals and uncover exclusive coupons. Compare prices and note which items are on a special deal. This ensures you're armed with the key information you need before you step into the store. Every sale you find and coupon you clip is going to reduce your grocery bill.

3—The List

Make a list of all the essential items you need for the week. Include all of your family's staple foods through your important household items. Consciously separate your "needs" from your "wants." This will keep your budget in check. Ask yourself, "Is this necessary, or is it just a fleeting craving?" This avoids impulse buying. Creating a detailed list gives you a clear roadmap to follow.

4—Organize Your List

Reorganize your list into logical groups. Use sections like produce, dairy, and household essentials. It helps you find your way around the store easily. This way, you won't wander down every aisle and make impulse buys.

5—Commit

Promise to follow your list strictly and resist tempting impulse buys.

6—Review

Assess your performance when you've returned. Check your final receipt against your original list. Think about what worked well and where you might have gone off track. Did you stick to your list? Use these answers to adjust your strategy next time.

Takeaways

1—A clear, detailed list helps you remember your priorities. It also keeps you from being distracted by tempting but unnecessary items. You've decided you are in control of your finances.

2—When you research sale ads and clip digital coupons ahead of time, you transform a routine errand into a strategic financial move. This preparation cuts your grocery bill. It also makes shopping quicker and easier. You're stretching every dollar.

3—An organized shopping list is like a well-planned roadmap. Organizing your list by store sections helps you stay focused. This way, you won't wander into aisles filled with tempting items. You're building long-term discipline that goes far beyond a single trip.

4—Leave once you've gotten all the needs on your list. Don't go back through the store and pick up all the other things you'd like or want and blow past your budget.

5—Avoiding premium and name-brand items can help keep your list lean and costs down. Choose generic or store brands instead.

These strategies all start with a simple grocery list. Preparation means control. A clear plan helps you focus on your needs. The changes you make in your grocery shopping habits will ripple across your entire financial landscape.

Chapter 8

Action 6--Cut Habit Spending

Problem with Liquid Cash?

New Habit for Banker?

I connected with a former investment banker. He wanted to get out of the rat race and cut his long hours. He wanted to do something on his own, so he started a blog and was writing for places to get some additional income. He was making much less money, so he knew he had to reduce his expenses heavily. He moved out of Chicago and cut his housing expenses.

Many afternoons, he bought himself a smoothie as a treat. He pulled the debit card charges for a few months and found he had spent $350 on smoothies each month. He knew he couldn't afford that habit, so he cut that monthly expense to $50 and saved $300 a month with that one decision. He saw that it was purely a "want" that he could not continue in making his career decision. He saw he had been blowing some of his higher pay on things that weren't important to him but had become a habit. Since he had been in an investment banking entity, he realized he was doing what former clients were doing rather than investing in his future. You can do the same.

The Seemingly Invisible Trap

You're running errands and, feeling a little sluggish, decide to swing by the drive-thru for a coffee. It's only $5, and in the grand scheme of things, it feels like a small indulgence. But as the days go by, you find yourself repeating the same routine. Then, a week goes by, and you start to do the math. You've stopped for coffee every day—five days a week, $5 per cup. That's $25 a week. You try not to think about it too much, but it has become a pattern. You may think of these purchases as vices. Examples are lattes, iced drinks, smoothies, muffins, pastries, candy, and cigarettes. Also included are items from convenience stores and drive-thrus.

A month later, you do the math again—$25 per week for four weeks. You're spending $100 a month on coffee. That adds up to $1,200 per year—all spent on something that's gone in a few minutes. That $1,200 could be used for something much more meaningful, like paying off a credit card or building a crucial emergency fund. You need to recognize how these small habits pile up over time. Instead of stopping at the drive-thru every morning, make your coffee at home and save. An occasional splurge is fine, but be mindful of how you are choosing to spend your money daily.

What Most People Do That Doesn't Work

We just had multiple big convenience stores open in Toledo from a chain named Sheetz. I went to one of their Grand Openings. They gave away teaser deals to get you to come in and spend. Specials included: 50 cents off each gallon of gas for a month, 2 free hot dogs, a free order of fries, and a free drink of any size. They also offered free coffee. This is a smart move since many people who struggle financially often spend too much in these places. The store hopes people build this spending habit into their daily lives.

Gas is a draw to a convenience store to get you inside and spending. Offering specials to upsize to a huge drink gets people inside regularly. For example, a bottle of water at my local convenience store costs $1.49. That's 12 times more than the price at Meijer, the big box store nearby. Think about how much waste that adds up to over time.

You may recall in a previous chapter I mentioned the Pepsi vs. Coke taste test I did in college. At that time, Pepsi was spending 5 cents ($0.05) on the drink materials while restaurants charged $1.49. The restaurants had huge margins on drinks, which continue today. Convenience stores are well known for charging well above other stores for their goods. They are designed to catch you at your most vulnerable—when you're in a hurry or craving a quick snack. They want you to spend money without thinking. You often pay a lot more for things that really aren't much more convenient. A little planning can make a big difference. This is a great item to cut heavily.

Why Habit Spending Doesn't Work

The problem with habit spending is that it's incredibly inefficient. You're paying a premium for things you could easily buy for much cheaper if you planned ahead. For example, a bag of chips or a candy bar from a vending machine can cost $1.50. But if you bought a whole box of those same snacks in bulk at a warehouse store like Costco, you'd pay maybe 25-50 cents each. Why pay so much more?

Since these moves seem automatic at times, you might not even realize you're doing them. Over time these "little things" add up. You probably don't realize how often you're doing it until you stop and add up the costs. You could easily spend $200 a month or more on unnecessary items. With many people living paycheck to paycheck, you don't have the luxury of wasteful spending. Every dollar you spend on convenience is a dollar not used to boost your financial health (opportunity cost).

What to Do Differently

The first step in cutting habit spending is recognizing how much you're spending. Having food delivered and similar habits popped up as new costs during the pandemic that should be stopped. When you grab a coffee or a snack, ask yourself, "Is this helping my financial goals?" This change in thinking helps you see ways to save. Consider how you can apply the savings to something practical, like paying down debt or building your emergency fund.

People have to quit thinking about such short-term, satisfying wants, and look into more long-term thoughts. Needs are the things that keep you alive—food, shelter, and clothing. Wants, on the other hand, are everything else. Convenience stores and drive-thrus are almost all wants, which is why they usually do well. I'm not saying you need to stop all the rewards you give yourself for doing well at work, school, or other activities. You can still treat yourself at a convenience store or drive-thru. But be mindful and limit how much you spend on these kinds of expenses.

Unfortunately, many people have grown up satisfying everything they want right now, and they don't look to the future. To reach your financial goals, you may have to break habits you got used to previously in life. Remember, every dollar matters, especially for long-term financial goals.

Why This Will Work for You

When you plan ahead and buy in bulk, you're taking control of your finances. Those extra savings can add up fast. You can use them for more important things. It allows you to stop living paycheck to paycheck, which is stressful. The power behind cutting habit spending is consistency. The cumulative savings are huge. It's like committing to a workout routine. You don't see drastic results after a day or two, but as you stick with it, the changes become undeniable. Those savings give you more financial freedom in the long run.

Achieving your long-term financial goals feels better than the quick joy of that convenience store latte. Paying off a credit card or watching your savings grow feels much better than the quick high from a bag of chips. Reaching a savings goal, cutting debt, or seeing your investment grow brings lasting joy.

10 Principles to Cut Habit Spending

1--Track Your Spending

Start by recording everything you spend on convenience items each week. Don't skip anything. You will be surprised at how quickly these little purchases add up. You can't fix what you don't see. Look at your total at the end of the week, then the month. That realization is powerful. It will kick-start your motivation to cut back.

2--Identify High-Cost Areas

Identify and total the biggest purchases. Also, get totals of the most frequent items and their costs. It's not just about how much you're spending—it's about where you're spending it. That snack could be costing you 6-8 times more than it would in bulk. These are targets to reduce and save.

3--Retailers Count on Your Impulse Buys

Convenience stores are designed to tempt you into impulse buying. The displays, shelf space, placement, and "specials" are temptations to buy. Retailers know that once you're in the door, you're more likely to buy things you hadn't intended to purchase. Noticing that you're being targeted is the first step to taking back control of your spending.

4--Delayed Gratification Leads to Greater Satisfaction

How long does immediate satisfaction last? Maybe an hour or two, and then it's gone. On the other hand, waiting for rewards can lead to much greater happiness. Financial security, travel, a new car, a home, and a comfy retirement all bring lasting joy. When you resist the immediate urge to splurge, you're choosing a future that's filled with bigger rewards. Think of it as putting down a small payment on the life you truly want.

5--Substitute Convenience with Bulk Purchases

Now it's time to make changes. Instead of running to the convenience store, think bulk. Warehouse stores like Costco and Sam's Club are your secret weapons. The per-item cost drops dramatically, and you can stock up on things you need. This one change could save you $1500-2000 per year. It's even lower cost when you catch it on one of their sales. Plus, buying in bulk saves time too.

6--Plan Ahead

Just set a little time aside every week to stock up on your bulk items and meal prep. Plan your grocery trips to pick up the things you know you'll need. Make it a habit to prepare meals in advance and pack those bulk items in your bag or car. Cook a batch of lunches, pack them in containers, and stash them in the fridge. These steps eliminate the temptation to stop at the convenience store.

7--Set Clear Limits on "Treat" Purchases

We all have those moments when we want a treat. You need to set limits on these non-essential purchases. Create a weekly budget for treats and stick to it. Setting boundaries will help you manage your urges. You won't feel deprived. If you withdraw only a set amount of cash and force yourself to buy these treats with cash, you won't overspend.

8--Every Dollar Has a Purpose

Money is a tool, not a reward. Every dollar you spend has a job to do, and if it's not working toward your goals, it's wasted. When you give each dollar a purpose, it begins to work for you. You can save for emergencies, pay down debt, or invest in your future. Being intentional about where your money goes is one of the most powerful shifts you can make.

9--Automate Saving

You've tracked your spending, identified areas to cut, and made the switch to smarter purchases. Maybe you cut out one convenience purchase a day or packed your lunch instead of grabbing takeout. Celebrate these small wins. Every time you say no to an impulse buy, you're building a new habit that will lead to bigger results. Every time you save money with these cuts, put it to work. Set up an automatic transfer to a savings account or toward debt repayment. You'll see your savings growing or debt reducing without even thinking about it. Over time, these small amounts add up.

10--Evaluate and Adjust Regularly

You need to check in with yourself regularly. Once a month, take a step back and review your progress. Are you saving more than you were before? Are there any areas where you're slipping back into old habits? Maybe it's time to set a new limit. Keep making tweaks, and keep celebrating your successes. Your journey is all about progress, not perfection.

Exercise—Cutting Habit Spending

1—Track Your Current Spending

For the next month, write down each time you buy something at a convenience store, drive-thru, or vending machine. Write down the amount plus what you bought. This might feel tedious, but when you see the total, you'll have a much clearer picture of what you need to change. Repeat this process for a few months.

2—Identify Habits

Review your log and identify the patterns. What recurring items are you buying? Take note of the items that you buy most often. Are they necessary? This is where you can start making cuts.

3—Find Bulk Alternatives

Find smarter, cheaper alternatives. For each recurring purchase, find a bulk option at a warehouse store and calculate how much you are saving.

4—Make a Plan

Stock up on the bulk items you've purchased and keep them within easy reach. Having your snacks, coffee, or meals already packed will reduce the temptation to stop for a quick fix.

5—Create a Budget

Assign a specific amount of money each month that you're willing to spend on convenience purchases, if any at all. This should be realistic. Don't try to cut everything out right away. Track how much you're spending throughout the month. At the end of the month, compare the actual amount you spent with your budget.

6—Continue to Improve

After one month, review your log and see how much you've saved by sticking to your new habits. Congratulate yourself on your progress. Now, take it a step further. Look at your log again and identify any areas where you can change to continue improving.

Takeaways

1—Little impulse buys can slowly drain your bank account. They can add up to a shocking total. Cut most of them.

2— Get a membership at one of the wholesale places or go to a big box store where you can buy snacks and drinks in bulk. Compare a few stores and get them at the lowest price. Use sales and coupons.

3—Breaking the habit of impulse spending requires a shift in your mind-set. Focus on long-term financial health instead of small purchases for quick satisfaction.

4—Tracking your expenses will make you aware of what habits you need to change.

5—Track the savings from the wholesale store versus the convenience store. Then, redirect those funds to a more meaningful place.

6—Look at whether you should be eating and drinking the things you are buying as a habit. There may be healthier and less expensive ways to get your snacks and drinks. You may be taking in way too many calories or poor ingredients.

Chapter 9

Action 7--Decrease Credit/Debit Card Usage

Only Swipe If You Are In Control

Careless Spending Leads to Bankruptcy

Around 2002, I had completed law school and was a licensed attorney. Since I had bid on and bought bankruptcy and foreclosure properties, I was looking to open a bankruptcy law office. I knew someone in that role and shadowed him to try it out.

We met with a new client wanting to file Chapter 7 liquidation. This means you pay what you can and everything else gets written off by the vendors that you can't pay. He worked at the local Jeep plant for many years. They had a lot of overtime for over a year, so he made more than $100,000 a year. Very good pay and benefits for unskilled work. That overtime had just ended, so he was back on a regular, full-time 40 hours/week pay. He couldn't afford everything he owed, so he was going to liquidate and walk away. He would keep his house and vehicle, but give back any other titled goods he had bought.

When he was making so much money, he bought a big motorhome that he rarely used because he worked 60-70 hours/week. He also bought a nice boat that he rarely used. He bought TVs and stereos, went out to eat/drink, and bought groceries, utilities, gas, etc. on credit cards. He put all of these purchases on credit with payments for several years. He could make the payments while getting so much overtime, but with the cut in his hours, he could not make all of the payments. He had minimal equity in these items, so he took the easy route and filed for bankruptcy. The Bankruptcy Trustee sold the titled items (motorhome and boat), and he got to keep the TVs, stereos, and other items that had no title.

Most items bought on credit cards are handled this way in bankruptcy. Credit card companies get paid last if there is any money left. Usually, there isn't, so they write off all of these purchases and the buyer keeps them. In this case, the motorhome, boat, and all of the credit card purchases had buried this family in debt. They couldn't control their spending when he was earning so much with overtime, so they had to start over. This is how loans and credit card spending can wreck a family's financial picture.

Don't Be the Average American Household

The average American household is sitting on more than $6,000 in credit card debt. It's dragging people down month after month. They're shelling out over $1,000 a year in interest. Imagine what could be done with that extra $1,000.[5] A solid emergency fund. A step closer to retirement security. It's a debt cycle that's designed to keep people stuck. Credit card companies count on this. A $50 dinner charged to a card with a high interest rate could take years to pay off if only the minimum payment is made.

I just did another house flip and pulled the credit card statement for the new furnace and A/C that cost $6,467. The statement shows that if I make the $235 minimum monthly payment and have no extra charges, it will take me 26 years to pay off the balance. I would pay $16,195, including

$9,728 in interest for a total of 250% of my initial charge. If I miss a payment due date, I would owe a $39 late fee plus my interest rate could be raised to the penalty rate of 34.65%. Wow! If you now applied that 250% rate to that $50 meal above, you would pay $125 for that basic meal. It's not a good choice.

What Makes Credit/Debit Cards a Problem

Credit and debit cards promise convenience, rewards, and financial flexibility. But for many people, they are a trap that is hard to escape. Many people don't see how their card use affects them until they face a lot of fees, high interest, and growing debt. Credit card companies fill mailboxes with pre-approved offers. They make it feel like it's a special chance. These offers are bait.

They offer sign-up bonuses and great perks. You can get cash rewards, zero-interest deals, or big discounts on your first purchase. It feels like free money. It's not. It's a strategy designed to get people hooked. Stores play the same game. At checkout, they offer immediate discounts if you open a store credit card. Saving 20% on today's purchase sounds great, but what they don't mention is the high interest rate that kicks in. College students and young adults, YOU ARE TARGETS. Screwing up your credit is not worth the T-shirt or mug they give you to sign up.

Credit cards make spending very easy. Studies show that people spend up to 100% more (double) when using a card instead of cash. Swiping a card doesn't feel like spending real money. There's no physical exchange. Just a quick tap and the transaction is done. Businesses know this. That's why they push credit card use.[6] Customers using cards tend to order more expensive meals, tip higher, and spend more on impulse buys. There's no moment of hesitation. That disconnect makes spending painless—which is exactly what credit card companies want.

Instead of questioning whether they can afford something, people think, I'll just put it on the card. "Wants" start masquerading as "needs." Small indulgences add up. Before long, people are spending more than they earn. Banks make this even easier by offering large credit limits, giving the illusion of extra money. A $5,000 credit limit doesn't mean you have $5,000 to spend. It means the bank will let you borrow that much but at a high interest rate.

Credit cards usually charge crippling interest. Most credit cards have 20%+ APR, with some climbing as high as 30%. That means for every $1,000 of debt, someone could be paying $200–$300 a year just in interest. And that's assuming they never make another charge. Missing a payment makes things even worse. Credit card companies love late fees. One missed payment can mean penalty APRs, late fees, and an even bigger balance to deal with the next month. Paying just the minimum each month hardly makes a dent. It only covers the interest. This keeps your balance the same and drags the debt on for years.

When credit card debt gets out of control, people start looking for ways out. But most "solutions" come with strings attached. Debt relief companies promise to reduce balances. They don't mention that payments are spread out longer. This means you end up paying more interest over time. It's a temporary relief, but a long-term financial drain. Credit scores take a hit, too. Writing off debt or changing payment plans can hurt your credit history. This makes it tougher to get mortgages, car loans, or credit cards with lower interest rates later on.

Some turn to bankruptcy, thinking it's the ultimate reset button. In some cases, it's necessary. But it's never painless. Bankruptcy stays on credit reports for up to 10 years. This can impact job applications, rental agreements, and loan approvals. And the emotional toll? Heavy. Credit and debit cards are tools that keep people stuck in a cycle. They encourage spending, borrowing, and paying interest over and over again.

Hidden Traps of Credit/Debit Cards

One financial emergency can set off a chain reaction that's hard to stop. A job loss, medical bill, or unexpected car repair forces people to rely on credit, thinking they'll pay it off later. Then interest starts accumulating, making the balance harder to pay down. Eventually, minimum payments aren't enough, and people use new credit cards to cover past debt. And the worst part? It all started with one bad month. The main way to avoid this is to build an emergency fund first. Having even a few thousand dollars set aside means you won't need to reach for a credit card when most unexpected expenses hit.

Credit card companies want you to spend more. That's why they constantly raise credit limits without being asked. A higher limit makes it easier to justify bigger purchases. Research shows that when people think they are earning rewards, they swipe more and make bigger purchases. "Buy now, pay later" options work the same way. They disguise debt as affordability, stretching payments out over months. Break this pattern. Use only cash for a week. You'll be shocked at how much more mindful you are about every purchase.

We've seen a commercial many times from National Debt Relief. It has many testimonials of people having over $40,000 in credit card debt. These companies know how to negotiate with credit card firms. They understand that credit card companies often lose the most when someone files for personal bankruptcy. They often pressure them to lower the balance to a more manageable payment. Many times, they extend the payment period as well. This hurts the customer further because they pay more interest overall.

It usually hurts their credit because they're having the credit card company write off this stuff as bad debt. It could help to use a debt relief company if you're in trouble. But, you need to research the company and understand the process first. These companies make the customer feel good when they reduce both the balance and the payment, regardless of the other terms.

Many assume debit cards are safer than credit cards. Debit cards take money straight from checking accounts. If you overdraft, you get instant fees, usually $35 for each transaction. That means a simple miscalculation can turn a $5 coffee into a $40 mistake. Debit transactions may not process right away, so you might spend money that's not there. And if fraud occurs? With credit cards, you can reverse a disputed charge. But with debit cards, stolen money is lost unless the bank chooses to return it. The safer approach? Use a separate checking account just for debit-card spending and keep a buffer amount in it. That way, there's no risk of overdrafting your main account.

Every dollar spent on credit card interest is a dollar that could have been working for you. Most people pay more in credit card interest than they invest in their future. Someone paying $500 a month in credit card payments at 20% interest for 10 years? That's more than $30,000 wasted. That money could have earned interest and compounded monthly.

Years ago, I was buying out a financial advisor at American Express. American Express sold its advisor division several months into our transaction. They noted that they were earning much more from the credit card division, so they wanted to focus on it.

What to Do Differently When Using Plastic

Credit and debit cards used correctly can be tools for convenience and financial gain. The key is controlling their use. Scan pre-approved offers and shred most of them. If you already have too many credit cards, it's time to clean house. Cut up and cancel any unused or high-interest accounts. The fewer open lines of credit you have, the less temptation you will feel to spend.

Credit should never be a way to buy things you hope to afford in the future. It should be a way to manage pre-planned, essential expenses. Use credit for insurance payments, utilities, groceries, or gas. These should be in your budget already. Never charge discretionary spending unless you can afford to pay it off that month. You must pay off the full balance every single month. No exceptions. Set up automatic payments. This way, your full balance will be taken from your checking account before the due date.

Gain control by switching to cash or a controlled debit account for daily spending. When you pay with cash, you physically see the money leave your hands, making it easier to stick to a budget. If you know impulse spending is a weakness, leave your credit cards at home. The less accessible they are, the less likely you are to swipe them. Set a weekly spending limit and stick to it. Once the cash runs out, spending stops.

Before making a non-essential purchase, wait 24 hours. This forces you to ask yourself: Do I really need this? If you still want it the next day and can afford to pay for it immediately—go ahead. But more often than not, you'll realize it was just an impulse.

If you're already carrying a credit card balance, the first priority is to cut up high-interest cards. No more charges. Now tackle what you already owe; focus on aggressively paying off the highest-interest card first. Once that's paid off, roll those payments into the next highest-interest card, and so on.

7 Practical Habits for Using Credit/Debit Cards

1—Use Their Money For Free

Never carry a balance. Outsmart credit card companies by never paying interest. Control your credit card use. If you stick to your plan, you can borrow money from the credit card company for free for up to 50 days before you pay it back.

2--Smart Credit Card Use

Only charge things you would have paid cash for anyway. Limit yourself to a couple of credit cards and monitor every transaction weekly.

3—Make Money Off Card Companies

Cash-back, rewards, and 0% interest can benefit you. But, you must pay off the full balance each month. A 2% cash-back card used for necessities like gas, groceries, and insurance can add up to $1,000 per year in free money. If you use a 0% APR offer, pay the balance off before the promo ends to avoid costly retroactive interest charges.

4—Remove the Option to Spend

If you find yourself justifying unnecessary purchases at Amazon, Target, etc., don't have a credit card linked to those accounts. Leave your credit card at home unless you have a planned, budgeted expense. Delete saved credit card information from online shopping accounts. A debit card with a set amount of money can also help—once the money is gone, you can't keep spending.

5—Strengthen Your Credit Score

A good credit score gets you better mortgage rates and car loans. If your score drops, lenders view you as a higher risk. Getting approved for a car loan, a mortgage, or a rental lease becomes harder and more expensive. To build and maintain a solid score: limit your credit charges to 30% of your credit limit (ideally, stay below 10%). Avoid opening multiple new accounts. If you have too many open accounts, close the ones with high fees. If you need a higher credit limit, call your issuer and request it.

6--Pit Card Companies Against Each Other

Credit card companies are highly competitive and willing to offer better terms if you ask. If you have a good payment history, you can negotiate better terms. A simple phone call can lead to better terms right away.

Contact your credit card company every 6 to 12 months. Ask for:

1. Lower APR

2. Waived annual fees

3. Higher credit limits

4. Rewards or cash back

If they won't budge? Let them know you are comparing offers from other companies, then switch to the best card. The trick is to be confident and persistent. If the first representative won't budge, ask to speak with a supervisor. A lower interest rate means more money going toward paying off your balance. It's worth the effort.

7--Use a Cash Envelope System

Some expenses are tougher to manage. Dining out, entertainment, and online shopping can quickly empty your bank account. Control these spending habits with a cash envelope system. At the beginning of each month, set aside a specific amount of cash for certain categories. Once that envelope is empty, you're done spending on that category for the month. This method forces discipline and keeps you from mindlessly swiping a card. When you're forced to use real cash, you think twice before making a purchase.

Takeaways

1—Only get credit cards that you can control and need. Having a credit card helps your credit score if you charge and pay it off timely.

2—Only charge those items that are "needs" until you can control your spending with a credit card. Do not charge “wants” on a credit card until you have full control over spending.

3—Credit card companies attract many people because they use cards for "wants." They often pay off balances slowly, leading to years of high interest costs.

4—Contact credit card companies and negotiate better terms annually. Be assertive with them, or go to another company.

5—If you manage your spending, use their money for up to 50 days free. Just charge the expenses you would normally pay. Then you get their cash back and other perks free too.

The best strategy? Get out of credit card debt as fast as possible, then never carry a balance.

Chapter 10

Action 8--Reduce Transportation Costs

Change This Area and Save Daily For Life

In most areas, it is normal to have a car. In big cities like Chicago and Manhattan, Uber, Lyft, cabs, and public transport can also cost a lot. Walking as much as you can will save money. Scooters and other small transportation devices can also be helpful. You may be able to share a car with roommates, your spouse, or a partner, or you may use a rental car company when needed. But if you need a vehicle...

Lease vs. Buy: Which Way to Go?

I don't suggest leasing a vehicle. Only consider it if there's a special deal. You should be able to compare the lease costs and see if it makes sense to lease vs. buy a reliable, used car that will last for years. Most lease agreements have mileage limits. They also include fees for extra wear and tear. This normally makes leasing more costly over time. We did find a lease bargain with my girlfriend, now wife, for a Toyota Camry while she was in law school. She didn't have a regular income and needed to stay on a tight budget. The dealer offered a great promotional education plan.

It had a two-year lease and cost about $120 a month, with maintenance included. This was back in the late 90s.

It was a new, higher-end Camry that was very dependable and looked fairly sporty. It worked very well for her at that point in life. We knew it showed a very high residual value at the end of the two years, so she could not buy it at the end of the lease. It had very low operating costs that worked very well while she was in law school. Unfortunately, she really liked the Camry while she had it and wished she could have bought it at the end of the lease.

Had we not found that deal, we were going to have her buy a 3-4-year-old, lower mileage Honda Accord or a Toyota Camry. One that had a great service history because they last for years with minimal repairs, and you could get them at a reasonably low price.

Maybe Consider Buying a New Car?

Owning a new car is far more expensive than most people realize. According to AAA, the average annual cost of owning and operating a new vehicle in the U.S. exceeds $12,000. This huge number covers more than just the payments on the agreed price. It also includes costs like depreciation, financing charges, fuel, insurance, and maintenance. What's alarming is that two big costs—depreciation and interest payments—often go unnoticed. Buyers usually don't see these expenses until they've committed to years of expensive ownership.

Depreciation alone can account for thousands of dollars lost each year. A new car loses about 20-30% of its value within the first year and continues declining rapidly in the following years. This means that if you buy a $40,000 vehicle, it might only be worth $28,000 or less after 12 months. This can happen even while you continue making full payments on the original price. Also, consider the cost of financing. Interest payments add up over time. This shows how a new vehicle can drain your finances quickly.[7]

What Most People Do That Doesn't Work

Many people buy cars as marketers and dealerships prefer: often, on impulse, and without thinking much about the long-term costs. They upgrade to a brand-new vehicle every 3-5 years, often stretching their budget to afford it. They justify it with the allure of a sleek new model, modern features, and a factory warranty. They don't see they are giving up financial freedom. Instead, they join a costly cycle of debt and payments. Each time they finance a new car, they take on another long-term, high-interest loan that drains their wealth over time.

Some people stretch their budgets to buy luxury cars they can't afford. They are attracted by prestige, comfort, or performance. A luxury car seems like a reward for hard work. But it's a financial burden. It needs higher insurance, premium fuel, and expensive maintenance. Leasing isn't any better. Many people keep leasing cars. They think they're saving money with lower monthly payments. In reality, they're trapped in a system where they're paying for a car they're renting, only to start over with a new lease every few years. It's a cycle designed to keep them spending indefinitely.

The biggest mistake? Ignoring the total cost of ownership and only focusing on the monthly payment. Dealerships know this, which is why they emphasize "affordable" financing plans. A car costs much more than its sticker price. You have to consider interest, taxes, insurance, maintenance, and depreciation. When people neglect regular maintenance, the problem compounds. Oil changes, tire rotations, and brake checks often get ignored. Then, a big breakdown happens. This can lead to a costly repair bill that could have been reduced.

Why This Doesn't Work

Some people never truly own their vehicle, always making payments on something that's losing value. Financing a car for five, six, or seven years can help you buy a nicer model. But by the time you pay it off, its value has dropped a lot. In many cases, they owe more than the car is worth before they even hit the halfway mark of the loan. People can get stuck in negative equity when they roll old car debt into new loans. This will make their financial problems even worse. Depreciation is the silent thief in all of this. Over time, they pay far more than what the car is worth, with interest charges adding thousands more to the cost. Instead of paying off debt, building savings, or investing, people funnel a large portion of their income into an asset that's losing value.

A Better Approach

Buying a slightly used, well-maintained vehicle is one of the smartest financial moves anyone can make. A car that's 3-4 years old has already taken its biggest depreciation hit but still has years of reliable life left. Some models, especially from brands like Toyota and Honda, are known for lasting well beyond 200,000 miles with minimal repairs. I've had my Toyota 4Runner for 15 years. Check vehicle history reports with a tool like Carfax. This will help you see if the car has been in major accidents or had big repairs. Look for a car with a solid service history, low mileage, and a great reputation. This way, you can enjoy a reliable vehicle without the high cost of a new car.

Look beyond just what's "affordable" for financing. Think about the whole financial picture. This includes the purchase price, interest, insurance, maintenance, and resale value. Short-term sacrifices, like driving an older but reliable car, lead to long-term financial gains. Paying in cash eliminates interest, but if financing is necessary, a short-term loan (no more than 2-3 years) keeps costs in check. Negotiate a low interest rate to get it paid off quicker. The longer the loan, the more you pay in interest and the longer you stay in financial bondage.

A car should be kept as long as possible—at least ten years, if not longer. A well-kept vehicle can last over 15 years. This saves you thousands on upgrades. Regular maintenance protects the resale value and prevents costly repairs. Store your car in a garage or covered area if you can. This helps protect it from harsh weather. It can slow down wear and tear and reduce depreciation. Shopping around, being patient, and knowing the fair market price gives buyers the power.

7 Core Principles for Reducing Transportation Costs

1—Negotiate Aggressively

Whether you're buying from a dealership or a private seller, negotiation is crucial to getting the best deal possible. Use tools like AutoTrader, CarGuru, Carvana, and Kelley Blue Book. They help you compare prices and find the fair market value of the car you want. Don't be afraid to walk away if the price isn't right—dealers often lower their price when they see you're willing to leave. Also, think about buying from a private seller. Prices are usually lower. But make sure to get a pre-purchase inspection from a trusted mechanic before you finalize the deal.

2—Minimize Unnecessary Driving

Reducing your driving frequency helps lower fuel costs, maintenance expenses, and wear on your vehicle. Plan errands wisely to cut down on extra trips. Also, think about carpooling, taking public transport, biking, or walking when you can. If you have two or more cars at home, consider whether you need all of them. Can a car be shared among family members so you can eliminate one? Reducing your overall mileage extends the life of your car and saves money on gas and maintenance.

3—Consider Hybrid or Electric Vehicles Cautiously

While hybrid and electric vehicles (EVs) can provide significant savings on fuel, they come with other factors to consider. Check battery life, replacement costs, and charging station availability before buying an EV. Some hybrid models may keep their value and need less maintenance. But others may cost more upfront, which can cancel out fuel savings. Check the numbers to see if long-term savings outweigh the purchase price. Also, look for used hybrid or EV models that have already lost value.

4—Flexibility in Vehicle Choices

Some car buyers lock themselves into a specific make and model, often influenced by brand loyalty or marketing. However, being open to multiple vehicle brands and models allows you to find the best deal and save thousands. Some vehicles keep their value better than others. Also, some brands provide more reliability for less money. Looking at similar models from various brands and being open to minor trade-offs can save you money. You won't lose quality or durability.

5—Timing is Key

The time you choose to buy a car can have a huge impact on price. End-of-year sales, holiday promotions like Memorial Day and Black Friday, and new model releases are great ways to save money. Also, buying from private sellers can save you thousands compared to dealerships. However, it does need careful vetting. If possible, start your search well in advance so you're not rushed into an expensive decision. Many people lose their negotiation power when they need to replace their car quickly. It's a long-term decision, so take your time.

6—Maintain Your Vehicle to Extend Its Life

Preventative maintenance is easy. Just follow the manufacturer's schedule. Check tire pressure often. Also, fix small problems right away to stop them from getting worse. Parking in a garage or under cover protects the vehicle from harsh weather, slowing rust and wear. I have seen people sign for $700+/month car payments for five years that keep them from paying off other debts and saving for retirement. Meanwhile, their expensive vehicle is sitting outside in the weather, depreciating quickly. Garages help keep your vehicle safe and valuable. So, think about whether you have a place to store your car when deciding how much to spend on one. In my area, I see many homes with 2-3 car garages, yet their cars sit outside because of too much stuff. Clean out the garage to get your car inside to reduce the rate of depreciation. Driving sensibly helps avoid hard acceleration and braking. This reduces wear and tear, so it extends the car's lifespan and boosts its resale value.

7—Use Price Comparison Tools and Negotiate

Dealers build plenty of wiggle room into their prices, expecting buyers to haggle. The best strategy? Be patient. Set alerts for price drops, contact multiple sellers, and be ready to walk away if the price isn't right. I make it a little competition and put saved search agents on sites like AutoTrader.com to find good candidates. Then I wait until I find the right buy. You can save a good chunk of money here if you're patient, do your research, and negotiate well. I've flipped several good cars by getting a good deal when I buy, then making money on the sale after I have enjoyed using the vehicle for a few years.

Exercise: Create Your Vehicle Cost Reduction Plan

1—Analyze Your Current Vehicle Costs Before Making Any Changes

You need to know exactly how much your car is costing you monthly and annually.

• Loan payments

• Insurance

• Gas

- Maintenance
- Registration
- Unexpected repairs

Also, consider depreciation. If your total costs are too high, cut back now.

2—Compare With More Affordable, Reliable Alternatives

Research the price of reliable used vehicles that fit your needs, but the total costs are lower. Some vehicles last twice as long as others while requiring fewer repairs along the way. Look for brands and models that regularly make "most reliable vehicles" lists from sources like Consumer Reports and J.D. Power. Focus on fuel efficiency, repair costs, and resale value. Make a grid of options with columns for costs along the top and vehicle options along the side. If you drive a costly vehicle, aim to switch to a fuel-efficient and reliable model. This change can help you save money.

3—Determine a Vehicle Budget

Decide on a maximum price for your next vehicle based on what you can truly afford. Your car should never keep you from your long-term financial goals. A good guideline is to keep your monthly vehicle costs under 10% of your gross pay. If you look at your take-home pay, aim for under 15%. I would try to stay below both of these. Start setting aside a fixed amount each month in a separate savings account labeled for your next car purchase. Try to make at least a 20% down payment, but hopefully more. Keep financing to 2-3 years max, or pay in cash if possible. If you can't pay in full, saving for a big down payment helps. It lowers the amount you need to finance. Setting a firm budget protects you from overspending.

4—Plan for Your Next Car Purchase

If you have a current car loan, make a plan to pay off an extra $50 or $100 per month toward the principal to get you out of debt quicker. If you're leasing, start preparing for your transition to a car you can own outright. Planning puts you in control.

5—Commit to a Maintenance Schedule

A car that's well taken care of lasts years longer than one that's neglected. Create a clear maintenance plan for your current vehicle. Set reminders to complete these tasks on schedule. Investing a little in preventive maintenance now can save you thousands.

Takeaways

1—Typically buy a good used, reliable vehicle rather than leasing or buying a new vehicle. Drive it until maintenance/repair costs get too high, then repeat the process.

2—Negotiate every cost related to your purchase. Include fees, interest, maintenance, trade value, etc. when purchasing a vehicle. Avoid amortizing fees and other expenses into your payment.

3—Compare repair costs with multiple vendors to make certain you're getting the best deal. Things that wear out regularly, like tires, mufflers, brakes, etc., can fluctuate by hundreds of dollars.

4—If money is tight, consider a reliable, conservative vehicle. It can save you thousands in operating costs.

5—Vehicles depreciate, so realize this is typically not an investment. This is an expense you're going to incur annually, and the vehicle value will typically go down. Getting a vehicle in a garage or at least under an outdoor structure with a roof will help extend its life.

Chapter 11

Action 9--Cut Health Insurance Costs

Very Important Area Now

I Don't Suggest Dying; Been There Done That

I play competitive pickleball and now teach it as well. Back on October 9, 2018, I was in the last game of a match when I dropped face-first on the court. Within seconds I had coded and was dead. My partner began CPR. An opponent, who is an M.D., checked my vitals. Meanwhile, a nurse from a nearby court hurried to clear my airway. My color came back so CPR was working, but the M.D. was not getting any vitals. The police arrived within three minutes. They took over CPR until EMTs came a few minutes later and continued the effort. I was not responding. They used an AED defibrillator twice (also known as "the paddles") to revive me. I was gone for about 10 minutes before they brought me back to life.

I am one of the lucky few who survived a widowmaker heart attack. At a young age, I didn't know I had two blocked arteries. My chance of survival was only 3% with the one blockage. The Left Anterior Descending (LAD) artery was completely blocked at 100%. The ramus intermedius artery was also significantly blocked at 80%. Thanks to the quick response of those who were present, I was resuscitated. Many people came up to me in the months after and touched me to sense what a miracle felt like. I believe I survived because I was young and fit. I was athletic and at my target weight. I also didn't smoke or drink. Plus, I had the right people there when I needed them. I had open-heart surgery (double bypass) two days later. A top-notch cardiothoracic surgeon from the Cleveland Clinic performed it. I left the hospital four days later feeling lucky to be alive.

I had over $225,000 in medical bills from that emergency. My insurance was a high-deductible plan with 100% coverage after the deductible was met. I had no co-pays or co-insurance, and I only had to pay the $5,000 deductible. Insurance paid the contracted rates for the remainder of my bills. Insurance saved me tens of thousands of dollars.

Insurance has changed. Now, companies pass more routine costs and initial hospital fees to patients. I would pay about $12,000 if that emergency happened today. That is why this chapter is very important. Can you afford to pay a surprise $12,000 bill? Do you have a big enough emergency fund to pay for that emergency? Many people lack those funds right away. They end up making payments for years, which can slow down their financial plans.

Don't Be Average

A 2023 study showed that the average American family spends more than $22,000 each year on health insurance and medical costs.[8] That's a staggering amount—often rivaling a household's mortgage or rent payment. Despite spending a lot on healthcare, nearly one in four insured people still avoid seeking medical care. They worry about the out-of-pocket costs. This means that even people with insurance often face tough choices. They must choose between their health and their financial stability. If you think healthcare is expensive now, just wait. Medical costs are rising every year—often faster than wages and inflation. Employers are shifting more of the cost burden onto employees, and government programs don't always cover as much as they used to.[9]

This paradox exposes a serious flaw in the system. Health insurance is meant to provide security, yet for many, it feels like a financial trap. High premiums, steep deductibles, and surprise medical bills make families cut back on care. They skip doctor visits, delay procedures, and avoid prescriptions they can't afford. The result? Minor health issues grow into major problems, leading to even higher costs down the road. When people are paying more than ever for healthcare but feel they can't afford to use it, something is deeply wrong. Understanding your health insurance options and costs is important. It helps protect your finances and well-being. Also, knowing how to cut unnecessary costs is key.

This chapter is about flipping that mindset. Health insurance is one of the biggest financial decisions you make annually. You could be throwing away thousands of dollars without even realizing it. Learn how your plan works. Compare options and make smart changes. This can lower your costs and ensure you pay only for the coverage you need.

What Most People Do That Doesn't Work

Many people make a common mistake. They just sign up for the default health insurance plan from their employer. They often fail to compare their options. Employers often provide multiple plans, and the difference in cost and coverage can be substantial. People think their employer picked the best plan for them. But the priciest option isn't always the best choice. The key is matching your plan to your actual medical needs.

Another mistake is blindly paying medical bills without reviewing them. Healthcare billing often has mistakes. Studies show many bills include overcharges, duplicate fees, or charges for services that were never provided. Most people just pay whatever bills they receive. Over time, this can add up to thousands of dollars wasted on incorrect or inflated charges.

People also assume that higher premiums mean better coverage, but that's not always true. While paying more may buy peace of mind, it doesn't necessarily mean you're getting the best value. Many people buy low-deductible plans they seldom use. They also keep costly insurance add-ons that aren't necessary. Many people don't know they can save a lot of money by switching to a high-deductible plan with an HSA. This is especially true for those who are generally healthy.

Even when opportunities to save are right in front of them, most people don't take advantage of them. Health Savings Accounts (HSAs) and Flexible Spending Accounts (FSAs) let you use pre-tax money for medical costs. This can save you hundreds or even thousands each year. But many people either don't know they exist or assume they are too complicated to use.

Some people skip preventive care to save money. They think this helps them avoid co-pays or office visit fees. When minor health issues are ignored, they can turn into major (and expensive) problems down the road. A routine checkup costs about $100. But if you ignore a health issue, it could lead to hospitalization, which can cost thousands.

10 Steps to Control Health Insurance Costs

1—Analyze your current plan

Many people sign up for insurance without fully understanding what they are paying for. Check your monthly premium, deductible, co-pays, coinsurance, and maximum out-of-pocket costs. Align your insurance plan with your actual healthcare needs, not just with what seems safest. The goal is to have the right coverage.

2—Compare available options

Employer-sponsored insurance is often the most convenient choice, but it's not always the most cost-effective. See if your employer has different plans. Also, consider private insurance and government programs. Check out ACA marketplace plans, Medicaid, or CHIP if you qualify. Maybe an HMO rather than a PPO or a traditional plan is the right move. Many HMOs cover more in-network, cutting deductibles, co-pays, and out-of-pocket costs. The plan that worked for you last year may not be the best option this year. Typically, fall is the time for Open Enrollment, which is the perfect time to reassess.

3—If you're in good health, consider a high-deductible health plan (HDHP) paired with an HSA

These plans come with lower monthly premiums, which can free up hundreds or even thousands of dollars a year. The key is that they are designed for people who don't expect to need frequent medical care. A benefit of an HDHP is the ability to contribute to an HSA. You can save and invest money for medical expenses tax-free. It grows tax-free and can be withdrawn tax-free for qualified medical expenses.

4—Pre-tax contributions don't stop with HSAs

If you can't access an HSA, see if your employer has a Health Reimbursement Arrangement (HRA) or a Flexible Spending Account (FSA). FSAs let you save pre-tax money for medical costs. However, you usually face a "use it or lose it" rule by the year's end. HRAs are employer-funded accounts that reimburse medical expenses tax-free. Some of these accounts reduce your taxable income, helping you save money on expenses you were going to have anyway.

5—Medical bills can be shockingly high

Never accept a bill at face value without reviewing it first. Contact providers before your procedures. Ask for price quotes and check what your insurance covers. Request an itemized statement to ensure you are only being charged for services you received. Many medical bills contain errors or duplicate charges. If you receive a bill that seems excessive, call the provider and ask if they can offer a discount, especially if you can pay in cash. Hospitals and doctors usually offer financial help. They may have sliding scale fees or interest-free payment plans. These options can lower your bills a lot.

When a healthcare provider bills for a service, they don't charge one fixed price. There is a "usual and customary" rate that has been negotiated between the insurance company and the medical provider. This means that the actual cost of a procedure or treatment isn't always what appears on your bill. If a provider charges $500 for a service, your insurance might have negotiated it to $300. So, that's the amount used for coverage. Understanding this can help you anticipate costs, challenge incorrect charges, and avoid overpaying. Many patients think their bills can't be changed. But medical prices are like car prices—they're often marked up. Check with your insurance company before paying any bill. Verify the negotiated rate. If something seems off, ask questions.

6—Vision and dental insurance can be helpful

Many people pay for these add-ons without considering whether they're getting their money's worth. If vision insurance costs you $250 a year but your only expense is a $100 eye exam, you're losing money. Instead, look at the cost of paying for routine vision and dental care directly. Compare that to what you would spend on insurance premiums. Some providers offer cash discounts for patients without insurance or their own plan, making it an even better deal.

7—Prescription drug costs vary widely, so shop around

Many pharmacies have discount programs to lower your medication costs. GoodRx helps you compare prices at various pharmacies. Ask your doctor about a generic version of your medication. It's usually just as effective as the brand-name one but costs much less. If you take regular prescriptions, check if mail-order services and 90-day supplies offer a better deal.

8—Use in-network providers

Out-of-network care can be exponentially more expensive, and in some cases, your insurance may not cover it at all. Before seeing a new doctor, verify that they are in-network. This is very important for hospital stays and surgeries. Many additional providers, like anesthesiologists and radiologists, may be involved. One unexpected out-of-network charge can lead to an exorbitant bill that derails your finances.

9—Preventive care saves money on healthcare

Most insurance plans cover preventive services like annual checkups, vaccines, and screenings fully. Catching potential health problems early can prevent expensive treatments down the road. Skipping regular checkups to "save money" can backfire, leading to bigger and costlier health issues. Maintaining a car is similar. Regular oil changes and tune-ups may cost a bit now, but they help avoid costly breakdowns later.

10-Build an emergency fund for unexpected expenses

Even with insurance, out-of-pocket costs can be unpredictable. A sudden illness, accident, or emergency procedure can result in thousands of dollars in medical bills. A dedicated savings fund for medical expenses can help you avoid debt and cover necessary bills. Aim to set aside enough to cover at least your deductible, and if possible, work toward saving for your maximum out-of-pocket costs.

Takeaways

1—Become knowledgeable about health insurance, and specifically your plan. Confirm what is covered, to what level, and who is covered. Customize your coverage to what you need.

2—Compare plans item by item so that you know the deductibles, co-pays, co-insurance, and maximum out-of-pocket costs. Know the costs and coverages of the main items that you expect to use every year. Make a spreadsheet. Use columns for different companies and rows for the main variables. This will help you compare options easily.

3—Consider an HSA, HRA, or FSA. Put money into these plans pre-tax so you spend on healthcare costs at a discount of whatever your tax rate is.

4—Preventative care is usually covered in full by insurance plans and is an investment in your health and controlling your overall costs. Factor in a portion of your emergency fund for emergency health issues.

5—Negotiate fees, billings, and payments on healthcare expenses. Many healthcare providers do not charge any interest on healthcare billings, so it may be wise to make payments to pay off medical debt.

Chapter 12

Action 10A--Decrease Housing Costs

Best Area to Save the Most

My 1st Home Purchase

I was in high school in the 80s and decided I wanted to buy a house to rent out. It was an obvious decision since I was making a whopping $3.50/hour working part-time at the local grocery store. Right? Ok, it was a stretch, but I was great at saving and stretching dollars. I had saved up a few thousand dollars to be my down payment. I lived in my small hometown of Fayette, Ohio, so the prices were low in comparison to bigger towns. We found a big house in foreclosure, going to the sheriff's auction soon, which was rare back then. I contacted the realtor, who never called me back. So I went to the house with my parents and grandparents and looked in the windows to do my best inspection.

My grandparents had mortgages on many houses nearby. They acted like a bank for others and agreed to do the same for me. I would pay the usual interest rate and have normal monthly payments. But I wouldn't deal with all the fees and paperwork banks require. Plus, I didn't have to qualify to get a mortgage. Since I was in high school, I didn't have the typical credit score or full-time job that formal lenders expect. An individual lender is usually easier and more flexible than a bank.

I made a budget that included the rent I could charge, the mortgage, repairs, utilities, property taxes, and insurance. I opted for a 15-year fixed-interest loan so I could pay it off quickly and minimize the interest that I paid. Since this was a sheriff's sale, I would receive a clean deed. All liens and debts from the previous owner would be wiped away after the sale. It functioned as my title insurance. Before I stepped into the courthouse on that April 21st day to bid on a house as a 17-year-old, I had a financial plan. It covered all of my income and expenses for this new rental property.

I got a hall pass, and my mom picked me up to drive to the county seat, Wauseon, Ohio, to attend the sheriff's sale. Shaking in my shoes, I bid on the home against the bank with the sheriff conducting the sale. He saw I was getting nervous late in the auction, so he had us take a break. I decided on my highest bid, which was just a few hundred dollars higher. He reopened the bid, I bid $100 more, and the bank said they were done. I had just bought my first house, with several more to follow over the next few years. I later found out that the bank manager called her boss during the break. They decided to lower the price to let me buy it. This way, they wouldn't be stuck with it. I signed the papers and returned to school. I slipped back into Government class, but no one believed where I'd been. Go figure.

Sadly, my first tenant passed all the background checks, but they turned into a nightmare. They stopped paying rent. They had the water and electricity shut off. They left old vehicles without plates. They left 50 Angora rabbits alone to starve. I found them and fed and watered them. Then, I got the Humane Society to remove them in the 90-degree heat. They left piles of old newspapers in the basement. The sump pump shut off due to the electricity being off. This caused a foot of water to flood the basement with the papers now floating. They let a freezer of meat spoil in the basement. It caused a terrible smell. We had to use a tractor to pull it out. I had the neighbors keep an eye out for them. I served eviction papers, filed a lawsuit, and garnished their wages. In the end, I recovered everything they owed me, plus interest. So, it all worked out. I continued buying properties and never had another big problem for over 20 years.

It was a valuable experience, and I am still thankful I took the plunge after proper planning. I learned how to fix many things in homes from all of these experiences. The tenants paid off my debt over time, and 20 years later, I sold the home for triple the price that I had paid.

2008 Housing Crisis Lesson

In 2008, the housing market collapsed, and millions of families lost their homes. What seemed like the American Dream turned into a nightmare. Families who worked hard for their homes now faced debt and foreclosure. They watched as everything they had built slipped away.

For years leading up to the crash, banks handed out mortgages like candy. If you wanted a house, there was a loan for you—whether you could truly afford it or not. Adjustable-rate mortgages (ARMs) start with low payments, but interest rates can rise with the economy. When that happens, homeowners face much higher monthly payments. Many stretched their budgets to buy their dream homes. This left no room for rate hikes or emergencies. Some people took out second mortgages or home equity loans. They used their homes like piggy banks to pay for renovations, vacations, or everyday costs.

Then the bubble burst. Home values plummeted. People owed more on their homes than they were worth. Job losses followed, making it impossible for many to keep up with payments. Foreclosure notices stacked up. Neighborhoods that were once thriving became filled with vacant homes and "For Sale" signs. The ripple effect was devastating.

Families were forced to uproot their lives. Credit scores were ruined, and entire communities suffered.

This housing crisis taught us a hard lesson. It shows what happens when people push their housing budgets too far. The lesson? Be conservative with housing costs. Buying the biggest house you can afford on paper isn't normally a great decision. When tough times come, breathing room in your budget can keep you in your home. It can also prevent you from losing everything.

What Most People Do That Doesn't Work

Many people treat home buying like a competition. How much can I get approved for? Lenders inform them of the maximum amount of a mortgage they can afford. Instead of picking a home below that amount, they spend their entire budget. They get the biggest house in the best neighborhood. Just because the bank says you qualify for a large loan doesn't mean it's a wise financial decision. A bigger home means bigger expenses that quickly add up.

New homeowners often fail to account for property taxes, insurance, HOA fees, maintenance, and utilities. When winter heating bills or unexpected roof repairs hit, they're blindsided. Home ownership goes beyond just paying the mortgage. It includes handling all the extra costs that come with it. The real cost of homeownership is far greater than what's on a loan statement. They assume that if they can just make the monthly payment, everything will be fine. If a family spends too much on their home and has no savings for surprises, one crisis can lead to financial trouble.

Some people assume that the first mortgage rate they're offered is the best they can get. The same goes for home insurance and even utility providers. Failing to negotiate or compare options can cost homeowners thousands over time. Lenders and insurers realize you may negotiate, yet most people don't. They settle too quickly and leave money on the table.

Once you get a home, it's easy to want to upgrade everything. You might think about remodeling the kitchen, finishing the basement, or redoing the bathrooms. Many homeowners spend tens of thousands on renovations. They often don't think about whether they can afford it or if they will get that money back. The reality is that most home upgrades don't add as much value as people expect. When those renovations are paid for with home equity loans or credit cards, they become just another source of more expensive debt.

7 Habits for Lowering Housing Costs

1—Regularly Review Your Budget

Monthly bills fluctuate, insurance premiums rise, and property taxes increase. To stay in control, review your housing expenses often. Make sure they fit within your budget. If your mortgage, insurance, property taxes, utilities, and maintenance costs eat up too much of your income, it's time to adjust. Many homeowners fall into the debt trap by using home equity like an ATM. Second mortgages and HELOCs (Home Equity Lines of Credit) look like quick cash. But they put your home at risk by using it as collateral for more debt.

Borrowing against your house can pay for renovations or other costs. But it also raises your monthly payments and financial risk. If the market dips or your income falls, you might end up underwater. This means you owe more on your home than it's worth or what you can afford. If you're renting, you can use many of the same search and comparison methods. These techniques help reduce costs related to renting.

2—Shop Around for Services

One of the easiest ways to lower housing costs is by shopping around for better rates. Many people sign up for a mortgage, home insurance, or utility service and never think to negotiate. That's a mistake. Lenders, insurers, and service providers frequently change their rates, and loyalty rarely gets you the best deal. Create a written checklist of variables, so you can run through the same items with each possible lender to compare them easily. Get into the habit of comparing mortgage rates every few months to see if refinancing is a good option. Every percentage point you shave off your rate translates to thousands in savings over time.

Check your insurance policy each year. Compare quotes from different providers. Also, consider raising your deductible. This might lower your premium, but be careful not to take on too much risk. Have a conversation with your agent about all of the levels of your insurance. Also, ask what other changes to your policy could reduce your rates. It is a risk-reward debate you can assess once you know the numbers. I have an umbrella policy that is an extra cost to me that could be eliminated or reduced if I needed to find extra money.

Assess the cable/internet/phone bill to see what changes could reduce that bill since it has grown over the years. If you have a landline phone, maybe that can be eliminated along with the access fees and taxes. I have found that there are more taxes and fees attached to this billing than any others.

For each of these services, if you don't get a good representative the first time, call a second time for a better representative. Encourage yourself, your spouse, and your family to think beyond their usual limitations. Explore new possibilities together. At least annually, review every single housing cost and formally renegotiate some. You can only gain by asking for reductions and making comparisons to competitors to get lower rates. This will build your negotiation skills.

3—Perform Preventative Maintenance

Neglecting maintenance is like ignoring the check engine light on your car. The problem doesn't go away—a small issue gets worse and more expensive. Simple habits make a big difference. Clean gutters seasonally to prevent water damage. Check for drafts around windows and doors to reduce heating and cooling costs. Change HVAC filters regularly to keep your system running efficiently. Routine maintenance is about avoiding large, unexpected repair bills.

4—Use Energy Wisely and Reduce Your Utilities

Your utility bills might seem fixed, but they're somewhat within your control. Small changes in energy use can lead to big savings over time. Lowering your thermostat a few degrees in the winter and raising it in the summer reduces heating and cooling costs. LED lighting uses a fraction of the energy of incandescent bulbs and lasts much longer. Other upgrades can also pay off. Smart thermostats adjust energy use without sacrificing comfort. Adding insulation and sealing air leaks keeps your home more efficient. Replacing appliances with energy-efficient models lowers water and electricity bills.

Here are some options that might help:

(a) If you water your lawn, cut back on watering times. Turn off the sprinklers when it rains or stop sprinkling altogether.

(b) Consider using a fireplace or a ventless gas wall heater.

(c) Lock in gas and electric rates for a year or more if they're lower.

(d) Use an electric reseller that buys in bulk to sell at lower prices.

(e) If an appliance breaks, check its utility use (natural gas, electric, or LP) to help choose a replacement.

(f) Use a budget plan to balance your costs, but keep an eye on your usage throughout the year. This way, you won't overpay or end up with a large balance at the end of the year.

5—Appeal Property Tax Assessments

Many homeowners just accept their tax bill without questioning it, but there's a good chance they are overpaying. Your property taxes are based on an assessed home value, and if that valuation is too high, so is your bill. Check your home's assessed value against recent sales of similar properties in your area. If your home is valued higher than comparable houses, you may have a case for an appeal. Contact your local assessor's office, gather evidence, and challenge the valuation. A successful appeal can save you hundreds, even thousands, of dollars per year. Our property taxes are high where I live, and I appealed and got mine reduced by $1,500/year.

6—Make Extra Mortgage Payments

Every extra dollar you put toward your mortgage principal shortens the life of your loan. It reduces the total amount of interest you will pay. You don't need to make massive lump-sum payments to see results. Even small amounts add up. Round up your monthly payment to the next hundred-dollar mark. Apply work bonuses, tax refunds, or any unexpected income toward your mortgage. If you get a raise, consider increasing your mortgage payment instead of adjusting your lifestyle.

7—Avoid Unnecessary Upgrades

Many people feel the urge to renovate their homes. It's easy to get inspired when you see others upgrading their kitchens, adding decks, or putting in fancy landscaping. But not all home improvements pay off financially. Homeowners often spend a lot on upgrades, but these don't always raise their home's value enough to cover the cost. Before taking on a renovation, ask yourself if it's necessary or just a "want." Focus on practical improvements that maintain the home rather than luxury additions. If you plan to sell in the next several years, research which upgrades add value to your market. A new coat of paint or small updates to the kitchen and bath are better investments. They often give you a bigger return than trendy remodels that don't pay off much.

NEXT!

Read the next chapter carefully. Make sure you understand it well. Then, decide how to move forward with the housing section. This area is crucial to focus on regularly. You can save the most money in your financial plan here. If it's a little scary, that is normal. Just get into it one step at a time.

Chapter 13

Action 10B--Mortgage Variables to Negotiate

Get Very Familiar with this Area

Resist the Temptation to Keep Up with the Joneses

Almost 33% or 42 million American households spend over 30% of their income on housing.[10] This limits the rest of their financial plans. When housing costs eat up too much of a paycheck, families are left with little room for anything else. For many, this means living paycheck to paycheck. A single unexpected expense or a temporary job loss can push them into a crisis. There's no cushion, no backup plan, just mounting stress and a growing fear of falling behind. Some turn to credit cards, racking up debt just to cover everyday costs. Others take out second mortgages or home equity loans, digging an even deeper financial hole.

Most advisors say to spend 30% or less on housing. Include all of your utilities, taxes, insurance, mortgage, and any fees in your housing expense number. I wouldn't use that as a hard-and-fast rule. Ensure you can comfortably pay the total monthly amount. Try to stay a few percent below it.

High housing costs lead to more anxiety and depression. People often work long hours just to afford their mortgage payments. This leaves less time to spend with family, friends, hobbies, fitness, and other activities. Feeling pressured to keep up can lead to poor financial choices. For example, some might take on extra debt. Others may delay important expenses, like healthcare or saving for retirement. Keep housing costs low. This helps you gain control, reduce stress, and build a strong financial future without a big mortgage payment.

Essential Mortgage Principles to Understand

A 30-35-year mortgage looks like a safe choice, but it has a big downside: cumulative interest. Over the life of a 30-year loan, you can easily pay double what you originally borrowed. A 15-year mortgage, on the other hand, keeps total interest payments much lower and helps you build equity much faster. The monthly payment is higher, but if you can afford it, you'll save tens of thousands of dollars over the long run. You can also have a 20-25-year loan.

If you're worried about the payment on a 15-year loan, you can choose a longer term. This way, you'll have a lower payment. But try to pay as if it's a 15-year loan whenever possible. Have all extra money in your payment applied to the principal of the loan, so you can pay it off early. Once you have a mortgage, refinancing it when interest rates drop can lower your payment. It also reduces the total amount you pay. A few percentage points might not seem like much, but over decades, the reduction will add up significantly.

Make certain you cover all of the costs of refinancing since Lenders are known for throwing in a lot of needless fees. You can and should negotiate heavily to eliminate or reduce fees. Minimize this long-term expense in every way possible. Avoid amortizing extra fees, as they will raise your total interest on the loan.

Let's look at an example so you understand how much the terms can affect your costs. You can use an online amortization application to obtain this information. I'm leaving out Private Mortgage Insurance (PMI) in my example. PMI often gets added to your monthly payment if your down payment is less than 20%. I'm also ignoring property tax and insurance escrows to keep things simple.

The table that follows outlines a $250,000 mortgage loan (the average U.S. mortgage). Section A shows options for a typical 30-year amortization, while Section B shows the options for a 15-year term. I used a 2021 average rate of ~3.0% APR during the pandemic era, and a 2025 average rate of ~6.0% APR with 0, 1, and 2 points to show what a difference these variables make. Study the figures in this table closely. Let them sink in. They shock most people. These should encourage you to allocate a good amount of time to decrease your costs.

As you can see, the interest rate makes a big difference. A person who borrows $250,000 at 3% for 30 years (Line 1) will pay $129,444 in interest. If you borrow the same amount for 30 years at 6% (Line 2), your monthly payment will rise by $445. You'll also pay an extra $160,151. Section B shows the impact on a 15-year mortgage. A person with a 6% interest rate (Line 6) will pay $68,974 more than a person with a 3% rate (Line 5). Shopping for the best interest rate is critical. Refinancing can be a smart move if you can secure a lower rate.

The term of the loan also makes a significant difference. Compare Line 2 to Line 6. Both loans are for $250,000 at 6%. The person who pays off the mortgage in 15 years saves $159,859 compared to someone who takes 30 years. With a 15-year mortgage at 3% (Lower Rate—Line 5), a borrower pays $228,833 less than with a 30-year mortgage at 6% (Higher Rate—Line 2). That's almost the entire cost of the home!

	Term	Interest Rate	Points Paid	Payment/Mo	Total Interest Paid	Total Amount Paid
	A					
1	30 yr	3%	0	$1054	$129,444	$379,444
2	30 yr	6%	0	$1,499	$289,595	$539,595
3	30 yr	5.75%	1=$2,500	$1,459	$275,216	$525,216
4	30 yr	5.50%	2=$5,000	$1,419	$261,010	$511,010
	B					
5	15 yr	3%	0	$1,726	$60,762	$310,762
6	15 yr	6%	0	$2,110	$129,736	$379,736
7	15 yr	5.75%	1=$2,500	$2,076	$123,685	$373,685
8	15 yr	5.50%	2=$5,000	$2,043	$117,688	$367,688

Let's take a moment to consider the impact of "points" that can be negotiated into your mortgage. These are lump-sum payments that you can make upfront to reduce the total amount that you ultimately pay on the loan. It's similar to making a down payment to reduce the amount that you borrow. But the points also lower your mortgage interest rate. As we discussed, a lower rate can greatly impact the loan over time.

One point typically reduces the interest rate by 0.25 percentage points. For example, 1 point could reduce a 6% interest rate (Line 2) down to 5.75% (Line 3). The cost of one point is equal to 1% of the principal. In our example, one point = 1% of $250,000, or $2,500. You can use simple math to calculate the cost of two points (2 x $2,500 = $5,000).

According to the previous chart, Line 3 shows that paying 1 point (1% of the principal, or $2,500) upfront on a 30-year mortgage lowers your interest rate to 5.75% from 6%. This change means you'll pay a total of $525,216. That's $14,379 less than the $539,595 you would pay without the point. So you can save nearly 6 times the cost of the 1 point. And the savings add up if you can afford to pay two points upfront. Line 4 shows 2 points = 2% of principal or $5,000 upfront would save another 0.25% on the interest rate. This results in a 5.5% interest rate. The total amount paid will be $511,010. So paying $5,000 upfront would save you $28,585. Again, you'll save nearly 6 times the cost of the 2 points.

Exercise

Since you can save more in this area than probably in any other, take action now. Using several hints in Action 10A, make a list of 10 specific actions you will start with to reduce your housing expenses over the next month. It will be worth the extra effort to attempt to get each of these reduced. After finishing each item in this category, set a calendar reminder to review specific items in six months. Make this a regular process to keep these expenses as lean as possible. Redirect any savings to paying down debt and investing for your future.

Takeaways (Actions 10A & 10B)

1—Spend below the 30% national average on all of your housing expenses. Target 20% of your income and see how close you can get. Make your target expense easily achievable.

2—Negotiate every expense included in this category. Mortgage rates, fees, insurance, taxes, and utilities all add to housing costs. So, it's important to negotiate these fees, as well as any others, at the start and regularly after that. Compare several lenders before you make a long-term commitment to a mortgage.

3—Make the largest down payment you can on your home. Then, check if you can negotiate points to lower your interest rate. Negotiate the fees as well.

4—You want a fixed interest rate mortgage so your payment does not change for the life of the mortgage. Avoid Adjustable Rate Mortgages (ARMs), variable rates, and balloon loans with increasing rates.

5—Get a 15-year mortgage, if possible. When choosing a 30-35-year mortgage, consider the total interest you'll pay during the loan's life. Hopefully, it encourages you to go in a different direction.

6—Make additional payments toward the principal balance. Use the extra income you gain from bonuses, gifts, refunds, and side jobs to pay it down faster. Paying off your mortgage early saves a dramatic amount of interest. You can then apply the money you're spending to other debts or add to your investments.

Chapter 14

Action 11--Reduce Education Costs

Avoid Student Loan Debt

Save on Local College Options

When I chose a college after high school, I knew that living in a dorm or apartment with roommates would distract me. I would struggle to stay focused and finish my schoolwork. I knew I would not do as well, which would limit my job options when I was finished. I attended Northwest State Community College, a nearby two-year technical school. I chose it because I could easily transfer to local colleges later. This way, I could complete my Bachelor's degree after earning my Associate's degree.
I found two people from my small town to commute with and share driving expenses. It worked well, and I finished my financial degree right on time. I couldn't find a decent job right away, so I continued there for a second, related degree in IT.

I stayed at my parents' home and worked at the grocery store that was within walking distance of our house the entire time I was finishing my first degree. I even had a couple of other part-time jobs to make some additional money these first two years. I found an accounting job soon after working on my second Associate's degree, and they let me have a flexible schedule to fit in classes. I transferred all my classes to Defiance College, a local school. I started as a senior but needed to finish my freshman classes. Those were the only ones I needed. This college was within commuting distance from my accounting job, and my supervisor worked with me to fit in my classes. I was still living at home and commuting, heavily reducing my costs of getting three degrees. Within a few months of starting the accounting job, I got promoted to a much better management role at 20 years old.

I avoided tens of thousands of dollars in room and board expenses as well as the meal plan expenses most incur. I paid a much lower cost per credit hour at the community college for three of my four years, saving thousands of dollars and avoiding debt. I worked to afford a car and gas so I was never in debt to get my education. I continued to get advanced degrees after my Bachelor's, paying tuition from earnings and through scholarships. I also was a Graduate Assistant who got classes for free and was paid a stipend for the hours I worked at the college, offsetting my other expenses. Additionally, I got paid to tutor a few students when I was going to be on campus. There are ways to minimize costs and earn income while pursuing higher education.

Student Loan Debt Crisis

Nearly 43 million Americans are carrying student loan debt that takes, on average, nearly 20 years to pay off. The average borrower owes $42,000, but many owe much more. Total student loan debt has soared past $1.7 trillion. It now surpasses both credit card ($1.18 trillion) and auto loan debt ($1.64 trillion). Think about that for a second. Student loans outweigh every other type of consumer debt, except mortgages.[11]

This level of debt is shaping the financial futures of an entire generation. Loan payments eat up income that could be used to buy a house, start a business, or invest for retirement. Many borrowers put off big steps like marriage, buying a home, and having kids. They do this because they can't afford them. Instead of saving for their future, they're trapped in a cycle of repayment for decades. The financial weight of student loans extends beyond individuals, too. With so much income going toward debt payments, the entire economy feels the strain.

Instead of putting money into a 401(k) or an IRA, borrowers funnel cash into loan payments. The lost years of compound interest add up, leaving them financially vulnerable later in life. Debt forces people to take jobs they don't love just to keep up with payments. It limits career changes, entrepreneurial pursuits, and the ability to take risks that could lead to financial growth.

What Most People Do That Doesn't Work

Many students take the usual college route. They rarely stop to ask if it's worth the cost. They assume there's only one way to do things—pick a school, take out loans, and figure out the rest later.

Many students pick a college for its reputation, sports teams, or friends' choices. They often don't think much about the cost. They sign on for tens of thousands of dollars in student loans without a concrete plan for paying them back. They ignore scholarships, grants, and work-study programs that could have covered many of their expenses.

Spending habits in college often make things worse. Instead of living frugally, students often choose costly options. They sign up for expensive meal plans, rent pricey off-campus apartments, and buy new textbooks. They rarely look for cheaper choices. They take out extra loan money not just for tuition but for living expenses, entertainment, and travel. These choices leave them with even more debt.

Why That Doesn't Work

Some people end up paying back student loans well into their 40s and 50s, making it harder to build wealth. Many students graduate with diplomas in fields that lack good job prospects. Often, these jobs don't pay enough to cover the cost of their education. When a graduate earns $40,000 a year but owes $80,000 or more in student loans, they quickly realize the math doesn't work.

The ripple effect of student debt is massive. Homeownership is delayed because lenders take debt-to-income ratios into account when approving mortgages. Without disposable income, saving for retirement gets pushed aside. Many students also lack basic budgeting skills. This results in extra expenses and overspending. Once they realize the damage, they're already buried under years of accumulated debt.

Ignoring financial aid options only adds to the problem. Many students think scholarships aren't worth the effort or that they won't qualify. This belief leaves thousands of dollars in unclaimed funds. Many people overlook work-study programs, employer tuition assistance, and alternative education paths. They often don't think to explore these options.

12 Key Habits for Controlling Education Costs

1—5-10 Year Strategic Plan

Failing to plan financially for the next 5-10 years before and during college leads to a harsh reality after graduation. Figure out what you're going to do and any education needed to do it. Next, if necessary, check out schools. Think about what you can afford and want to pay. Look into financial aid options too. A solid plan should also have an exit strategy. This means figuring out how to repay student debt, how long it will take, and what income you'll need to live comfortably while making payments.

Money disappears fast in college if you're not keeping track. Small daily purchases—like coffee, snacks, and streaming subscriptions can quietly drain your bank account. Making budgeting a daily habit keeps spending under control and prevents financial surprises. Setting up a simple system to track where every dollar goes can be life-changing (see Actions 1 and 2).

Using a budgeting spreadsheet or app can help organize spending into categories. Setting a weekly limit on non-essential spending helps you make smarter financial choices. For example, it encourages cooking at home. Textbooks can be rented or bought used instead of purchased new. Look for free or cheaper options for transportation and entertainment. This can help your money go further.

2—Evaluating Your Return on Investment (ROI)

A college degree is an investment. Like any investment, it needs to have a solid ROI. Some degrees justify a high tuition price because they lead to well-paying, in-demand jobs. Degrees in engineering, computer science, finance, and healthcare often lead to good jobs. They usually come with competitive salaries. These degrees tend to offer a high ROI, meaning the cost of education is worth it based on future earnings. There are a few exceptions where you can take out loans because the ROI for those particular roles (e.g., Medical Doctor) is in demand and they pay a high income. However, degrees in fields that earn less or have few job options, like some liberal arts or niche creative areas, might not be worth the loans.

Students should check the median salaries for the careers they want. Then, they should compare those figures with the total cost of their degree. This means you should sit down and outline the full cost of attending school. Include tuition, housing, books, transportation, and daily expenses. If a career path doesn't provide a clear path to financial stability, it's worth reconsidering whether that degree is the best option. Is there a way to enter the field with a more affordable education path or make it a side gig?

3—Research and Apply for Scholarships Regularly

Most students don't apply for enough scholarships, often assuming they won't qualify or that it's not worth the effort. But every dollar earned in scholarship money is a dollar that doesn't have to be borrowed and repaid with interest. Make applying for scholarships a monthly habit. Do this during your junior and senior years in high school and throughout college.

Set aside time each month to find and apply for new scholarships. This keeps opportunities coming. Exploring scholarships beyond academics can reveal surprising funding options. Many awards recognize community service, leadership, specific majors, and unique personal backgrounds or hobbies. Applying for smaller scholarships can pay off. Many students ignore these chances, so the competition is often less than you might think. It is estimated that over $100 million in scholarships go unclaimed yearly, while another $2 billion in grants go unclaimed.

4—Maximizing Free and Low-Cost Education

Many students think a four-year university is the only path to success. But there are many ways to earn a degree without this route. Community colleges, online programs, and employer-sponsored education can lower costs. They still offer the same credentials.

Community college is an underrated option. A two-year Associate's degree or general education credits at a fraction of the cost of a university can save thousands. Many students move from community college to a four-year university for their last two years. They earn the same degree as those who stayed all four years, but at about half the cost.

Most universities offer online courses and accelerated programs at lower tuition rates. This lets students work while they earn their degrees. Some schools offer competency-based programs. In these programs, students can finish courses at their own pace. This may help them finish quicker and save money. Also, some companies provide tuition reimbursement for employees. This lets students earn a degree while working, often without accumulating debt.

5—Graduate in Fewer Years

Every additional semester in school means more tuition, fees, and living expenses. Reducing the number of years in college can save thousands. Finishing faster doesn't mean hurrying. It means being smart about how you earn credits. While in high school, take college credit classes (called College Credit Plus in Ohio) for FREE and get a head start on your degree. I know a few people who had a full Associate's degree done when they graduated from high school. Taking Advanced Placement (AP) or dual-enrollment courses in high school helps students begin college with credits already earned.

Enrolling in the maximum number of credits per semester can shorten the time needed to graduate. Taking summer or winter break classes can further speed up progress. Some schools offer credit for work experience or allow students to test out of certain classes. The goal is to graduate without paying for extra semesters that aren't necessary.

6—Paying as You Go

One of the best ways to avoid student loan debt is to pay for college as you go, rather than relying on loans. Even if covering the full cost upfront isn't possible, earning money along the way can drastically reduce the amount that needs to be borrowed. Working part-time while in school helps cover tuition, books, and living expenses. Paid internships allow students to earn money while also gaining valuable career experience.

Some students pick freelancing or side gigs. They might tutor, do graphic design or social media, write, or resell items online to earn money. It makes post-graduation job hunting easier with work experience already on a resume. Paying just a few thousand dollars out-of-pocket each year can significantly reduce student loan burdens. Every dollar paid up front is a dollar that won't accrue interest later.

7—Network & Job Shadow

Getting a degree is only part of landing a great job after college—connections matter just as much. The earlier students start networking, the more opportunities they create for themselves. Career fairs, student organizations, and connections with professors can lead to internships and job offers.

Reaching out to professionals in the field and asking to job shadow or meet for coffee can lead to valuable advice, mentorship, and potential opportunities. Many companies prefer to hire from their pool of interns, so interning early—even if unpaid at first—can lead to paid positions later. The sooner networking becomes a habit, the easier it is to transition from student life to career life.

8—Creative Housing and Living Cost Reductions

Tuition isn't the only major expense in college; housing and living costs can be just as overwhelming. Living at home for the first couple of years can be a huge money saver, avoiding rent, utilities, and meal plan costs. If this isn't an option, renting a room instead of an entire apartment can cut housing costs significantly. A few students take it a step further—buying a small home with financial help from family, then renting out rooms to cover housing costs.

Other ways to cut costs are meal prepping instead of buying pricey dining plans. You can also use public transportation or a bike instead of getting a car. Finally, consider buying used or digital textbooks.

9—Develop an Entrepreneurial Mindset

Not every college student needs to rely on a job to make money. Thinking like an entrepreneur can lead to creative ways to generate income, reducing reliance on loans. Small side businesses can provide enough extra cash to help pay for school.

Selling skills online—such as graphic design, writing, tutoring, or video editing—can create a steady stream of income. You can make extra money by renting unused items, flipping thrift store finds, or offering services like pet-sitting or lawn care. These small efforts can add up over time. Some students turn their passion projects into businesses. They might create handmade goods or develop apps. An entrepreneurial mindset means learning financial independence early. It's about creating choices beyond regular jobs and staying out of the paycheck-to-paycheck cycle.

10—Alternative Paths to High-Paying Careers

A four-year college isn't the only way to build a successful career. Many alternative education paths lead to high-paying, in-demand jobs—often with far less debt.

Trade schools provide focused training in areas like HVAC, welding, plumbing, and electrical work. These careers can pay $50,000-$100,000+ a year. Plus, the schooling costs are low. Apprenticeships let students earn money as they learn. They gain real-world experience and avoid tuition costs. Technology certifications in areas like coding, cybersecurity, or IT administration can lead to high-paying jobs. You don't always need a traditional degree for these roles.

Some students even find that entrepreneurship or self-employment is the best financial path. You can learn a marketable skill and build a business—like digital marketing, real estate, or freelancing. This path can lead to financial independence, all without going to college. The key is to focus on earning potential and job demand rather than assuming a traditional degree is the only route to success.

11—Smart Student Loan Management

The goal of a loan should always be to borrow as little as possible and pay it off as quickly as possible. Federal student loans should always be the first option before turning to private loans. Federal loans have lower interest rates and better repayment options. They include income-driven repayment plans and possible loan forgiveness programs.

Students should only borrow what they absolutely need—not extra money for unnecessary living expenses. Taking a part-time job, using scholarships, and cutting costs can lower loan balances. Paying some principal and any interest while still in school, if possible, prevents loan balances from growing.

After graduation, the focus should be on aggressively paying off loans instead of making minimum payments for decades. Refinancing at a lower interest rate, making extra payments, and using salary increases to pay off loans faster can save thousands in interest.

12--Additional Ideas for Avoiding, Minimizing, and Paying Off Debt

(a) Buy a foreclosed home, fix it up, and rent rooms to cover your costs;

(b) Aggressively apply for fellowships, tutoring, teaching assistants, etc.;

(c) Manage your income and expenses like I do a turnaround. Stretch every bit of income, add income streams, eliminate or reduce any expense possible, and increase your cash flow. I developed a contest schools can use to train students. E-mail me if interested;

(d) Consider the military to get free tuition;

(e) If you or a parent works for the college you're attending, you may qualify for free or reduced tuition;

(f) You, your parents, or your grandparents can invest in a tax-advantaged college plan, like a 529 or Coverdell. You can start years before college, which helps you benefit from compounding.

Exercise: Build Your Higher Education Plan of Attack

Research three potential career paths that interest you. Look at expected salaries, job demand in your geographic area, and growth potential. Identify three schools that offer your chosen degree at an affordable tuition rate. Find five scholarships or grants that match your background and apply for them. Create a budget for your education. Estimate all expenses. Compare this total to potential earnings from part-time jobs or internships. Choose at least three specific strategies you will use to minimize debt and pay as you go.

Takeaways

1—Have a strategic plan and an ROI before committing to any schools and loans.

2—Know whatever field you're going into is what you really want to do long-term. If you're going to commit this much time and money, be confident it's the right path.

3—Do everything you can to avoid any loans and to pay as you go.

4—Look at alternatives to college, like technical education. Trades are another good option.

5—Do what is best for you and what makes you happy, not just what you think others want you to do, or what makes you look impressive.

Ultimately, stretch your mind and get creative to avoid debt. These habits aren't just for cutting college costs—they build financial discipline for life. The more students focus on budgeting, working, saving, and cutting unnecessary expenses, the less likely they are to have debt.

Chapter 15

Action 12--Pay Off Debt with Savings

Take Advantage of Your Hard Work

What's Next?

As soon as you start saving money with these Actions, use your new savings to pay down debt.

Let Me Repeat That

As soon as you start saving money with these Actions, use your new savings to pay down debt. This is when you start making changes to better your future. If you have no debt, invest all of your new savings. Consider a Roth IRA, in addition to your Roth 401k or Roth 403b at work. You can also look into a Solo 401k if you have a side business. ETFs are great for long-term growth and compounding your money. The younger you are, the better for compounding long-term.

Negotiating Mindset Shift

Sarah never thought of herself as a negotiator. She was a single mom, juggling work, bills, and raising two kids on a tight budget. Every month, it felt like her paycheck disappeared. When she first heard the idea of negotiating her bills, she laughed it off. Calling her internet provider for a discount felt scary and a bit embarrassing. What if they said no? What if they thought she was being cheap?

But one day, staring at another sky-high bill, she decided to try. She called her internet provider, took a deep breath, and simply asked, "Is there a better rate available?" To her surprise, they knocked $20 off her monthly bill on the spot. Encouraged, she tried again—this time with her car insurance. After a short conversation and mentioning a competitor's lower rate, she saved another $300 a year. After she negotiated a lower medical bill plan, she made a big discovery. She had saved over $3,000 without changing her lifestyle.

Negotiating became a habit. She called every service provider she could think of, always asking the same simple question: Is that the best you can do? Her confidence grew with each call. She finally applied the same mindset at work. She negotiated a raise, which she had never thought possible before. By overcoming the fear of rejection, she changed her entire financial reality. She didn't need a second job or extreme budgeting tactics. She just needed the courage to ask. And that single shift in mindset made all the difference.[12]

Assertive Debt Repayment

Taking on debt for the right investment reasons with well-calculated risk may make sense. But it's important to be protected from being overleveraged or buying in too high to the point that the debt exceeds the market value of the investment. That is what caused the 2008 financial crisis and left people's houses in foreclosure.

In high school, I began buying homes. I took on debt, but I got good prices. I built equity in those homes. Plus, I had short-term fixed mortgages. My renters helped pay them off each month. I ended up buying 10 homes over the first few years while I was investing in my small town of Fayette, Ohio.

I negotiated the purchases and bid at auctions to buy them. I did many of the improvements myself and with the help of my family and other local contractors. I helped the contractors to keep my costs down. I also learned their trades so I could handle repairs and improvements next time. This allowed me to control my costs so the rent covered most of my costs.

I handled all landlord tasks. I wrote tenant applications, rental agreements, and eviction papers. I took my first tenant to small claims court. I presented my case, won a judgment, and garnished his wages. I made sure he paid every penny he owed me, plus interest. It's interesting what you can force yourself to learn and complete when you need to keep your costs under control. I also did all of the banking, paying expenses, taxes, etc.

I used gifts, bonuses, side work, and other income to pay extra on my mortgages. This helped me pay them off faster and reduce interest. I paid off my 1st mortgage in 8 years and kept it for over 20 years, ultimately selling the property for 3X what I paid for it. I used the rent from paid-off properties to pay down the remaining mortgages. In the end, I paid off all the mortgages. I then decided to switch from residential rentals to self-storage. I strategically sold one or two residential properties each year. This allowed me to control the capital gains taxes I paid when I sold them well above my cost basis.

Suggested Process for Paying Down Debt

Pay off the debt with the highest interest rate first. This is typically credit cards. It will save you the most money in the shortest time. Alternatively, you could choose the one with the lowest balance. Paying it off can boost your confidence and help you tackle more debt. You'll have to decide which route to take based on your level of motivation. Decide and take action. You can switch methods if you start with the higher interest rate. You might see that you need some motivation to move ahead. If so, pick a small balance loan and pay it off.

Consider debt consolidation and refinancing. They may be able to lower your overall debt and interest rates. But realize that you don't want to increase the interest rates on any of your loans as part of the consolidation. Do the comparison calculations before making moves.

As an example:
Let's assume John and Janet Clark, with no kids, have a combined $6,000 in net disposable income per month. They have the following loans totaling $3,035/month:

1) $25,000 @ 5% fixed interest at $265/month for 10 years—Student Loans

2) $5,000 @ 19% variable at $50/month until paid off—Old Credit Card Debt

*Assume all new monthly charges are paid off every month.

3) $29,000 @ 6% fixed at $560/month for 60 months (5 years)—Car Loan #1

4) $15,000 @ 7% fixed at $360/month for 48 months (4 years)—Car Loan #2

5) $4,000 @ 0% fixed at $50/month until paid off—Old, Unexpected Hospital Expense

6) $5,000 @ 5% fixed at least $100/month payment, as they can afford it until paid off—Personal Loan from parents for wedding/honeymoon costs

7) $10,000 @ 4% fixed at least $250/month until paid off—Personal Loan from grandparents for side business start-up

8) $200,000 @ 3.5% fixed at $900/month for 30 years—Home Mortgage

9) $20,000 @ 6.25% variable at $400/month until paid off—Home Equity Line of Credit for a new kitchen

10) $4,500 @ 5.75% fixed at $100/month until paid off—Personal Loan from sister for used boat

For this example, I am ignoring whether I believe these are debts they should have incurred with their financial picture. I'm also assuming that they are not filing for bankruptcy. They have some savings that would cover a few months of living expenses. Therefore, we'll assume that they have the minimum emergency fund needed.

Their living expenses are $2,300/month (which includes the minimum contributions to their 401(k) account to get the company match). So, they have $665 extra each month. They can use this to pay down debt, boost their emergency fund, or add to an investment account.

Here's one way of tackling their situation loan by loan. They have too many loans and too much debt for their income. So, they need to reduce some of that debt quickly. They should start by making a schedule (it's easier with a spreadsheet that can be modified), listing all debts with their current balances. Also, confirm loan terms, interest rates, and payments. This will help them create a strategic payoff plan.

At the beginning, they incurred $200,000 on their mortgage and $117,500 on other debt. But they have been paying off the loans, so the current outstanding debt is lower. A basic amortization application online (i.e., Calculator.net or Amortization-calc.com) will show how long it will take to pay off each loan.

After understanding the current debt, the next step for them is to reach out to each creditor. They need to negotiate firmly for a reduced balance, lower interest rate, and better terms. They can tell these creditors that they are very committed to getting out of debt, but need their help. The Clarks should fully update their spreadsheet once they have all the final figures.

Here are some starting ideas:

#1 Some student loan debt is being forgiven entirely, so start with that goal and negotiate from there. Working for specific entities can also get your debt forgiven. Research options. Make the calls.

#2 Start with credit cards that have high interest rates and get them paid off. Limit new charges as much as possible. Use all of the excess money available each month to pay off this credit card debt, and never carry a balance again.

#3 If the car loan can be paid off without penalties and there is a cheaper, reliable option, get this debt reduced heavily. Cut your payment a lot. Consider a less expensive option for transportation.

#4 If you can pay this car loan off without penalties and there is a cheaper, reliable option, get this debt reduced. See if you can cut your payment. Get a lower-cost, reliable used car. Consider if you can get along with only one car if you live in an area with public transportation. Carpool?

#5 Medical providers may be willing to write off old debt, especially if payments have been made over time. It is worth negotiating. At the very least, a discount may be available in exchange for a lump-sum payment.

Maybe if you make several payments by a specific date, then they will write off the balance.

#6 Talk with your parents (lender) about the loan and get creative about what they would do. Propose reducing or cutting out all interest, reducing the balance, writing it off as a gift, requesting debt reduction as holiday gifts, providing services for them in return for debt reduction, etc.

#7 Re-assess your side business and its future. Get it producing net income and a good ROI, or see if it's time to shut it down and pay back the loan. Maybe your grandparents (lender) will reduce it or forgive the debt balance.

#8 Assess your mortgage and consider refinancing. If the rate is good, you may need to leave this as is and continue to watch offers. Address it last, but do assess it for a better option.

#9 If you can abandon the project or reduce it to needs only and repay all or some of the loan, do it. Since this equity loan is variable and has a higher rate than others, prioritize paying off this loan earlier than the others.

#10 Sell your boat and pay off the loan. When someone has too much debt, carrying a loan for items like boats and recreational vehicles is a luxury they cannot afford. At a minimum, get it reduced heavily so it can be paid off soon.

This is not the only way, but one way to take action now, which is the key. You can also do some side work for a creditor or anyone else. Then, use the income to pay down your loan balance. Other options include debt consolidation at a lower rate and buying good used cars for less money.

Exit Plan Per Loan

Get an exit plan for every loan. Try to reduce the debt or pay off the loans in creative ways as quickly as possible. Create a master plan with detailed numbers and dates to develop a debt-free target date in the future. Put the time in and take action now to aggressively start the process. Stay focused and persistent. A little sacrifice now will pay off multiple times in the future.

Take a Break and Reward Yourself

Reward yourself in some small way for each loan you get paid off. Recognize your accomplishment as you progress toward your debt-free day. Plan a bigger celebration for your all-debts-except-mortgage-free day. Do the same for your debt-free day. These are great goals to reach. And once the debt has been eliminated, the financial freedom will be worth all of the effort. The former payments can then be invested in income-producing accounts. This will help you build security and wealth.

Chapter 16

Final Action--Draft Your Plan

Put All of These Techniques in Action

You Did It! You made it to the end.

You've done something most people never do. You've gone from hoping things might change...to taking real steps to make them change. Congratulate yourself on making it here. This is a huge step to help you build a better financial picture. Now is the most crucial time. TAKE ACTION NOW! This is the key to everything I've shared to help you get a much higher net income.

Take Your Next Step Now

Go to Amazon and purchase the accompanying Common Cents Workbook. This companion tool will guide you through all 11 Actions. You'll complete the process step by step. It's the bridge between knowledge and implementation. It could mean the difference between "I read the book" and "I changed my life." Use it to build your plan, track your progress, and accelerate your results. You can also go old school. Write your plan on lined paper. Or use a Word document or Excel spreadsheet that you can easily change.

Get Started NOW!

Decide what your first Action is, then your 2nd, then your 3rd, or decide to attack two or three at once. I still recommend you get through Actions 1 and 2 at the beginning so your whole plan is accurate. When you track every dollar, find money leaks, cut wasteful spending, and make a plan for your life, you begin your financial turnaround.

Make A Full Plan

Plan out when you will complete every one of the 11 main Actions. List the first 5 steps you'll take per Action in your overall plan. This is your Master Plan of Attack. Take some time to lay it out in detail so you can refer to it regularly. Put projected dates that you will complete each of the Actions. Make them assertive dates so you can continue to move forward. This won't be theory anymore. It will become transformational. Remember, this journey isn't about perfection—it's about progress. The quicker you make these changes, the sooner you can cut your debt and start investing in your future.

Financial Advisor Caution

I've terminated several "financial advisors" over the years. They didn't advise much or actively manage my investments, but they still charged their fee. After years of working with different advisors and being one myself, I gave up. Now, I manage most of my resources. It takes longer, but I've gained a higher return on investment (ROI) than any licensed and trained advisor I've worked with. I know many won't want to do this, but I recommend checking your investments often. This helps you understand what you own and how it's performing against the market. Then talk with your advisor if you are concerned and modify it.

You'll find most are 100% commissioned salespeople. They invest your money in passive funds that are rarely reviewed or changed. Yet they charge ~1% or more annually while letting your investments stagnate. They want as many customers as they can get because their total income grows with more customers. Consider learning how to invest in mutual funds and ETFs. Then actively manage some of your investments. Compare your ROI to your advisor's ROI and see how you've done. At the very least, ask friends and family for a referral to an advisor who has done well for them. Interview a few advisors until you get comfortable with one. There are lots of good questions online for interviewing advisors. If you don't like the answers, move on to the next one. Realize you are paying them to manage and grow your money for you.

Sigh of Relief

Picture this: six months from now, you're no longer dreading the first of the month. You've paid off another chunk of debt. Your emergency fund is growing. You're sleeping better. Smiling more. You're not just scraping by—you're building a future.

This is a whole new and improved future, but taking daily action is the only way it happens quickly. You care the most about your family and its resources, so you need to change how you are using your resources now. Stretch every dollar, making each one count.

I leave you with the same thought I had my wife remind me of when I was nervously being wheeled into the operating room to have open heart surgery two days after flatlining.

You've got this, and I've got your back.

How Jeff Can Help?

Contact Jeff For Assistance

Some know me as The Turnaround Guy. It's a fitting title because I have helped several companies turn around and survive. Some have transferred to new owners or gone out of business in a planned manner. This avoided a fire sale or just closing the doors without notice. I've been trained in business turnarounds, and I think I like the adrenaline. It's usually a very daunting task, and I am competitive, so I take it as a personal challenge. Most of the time, I get contacted too late. By then, the company is almost out of cash, and it's too hard to fix the situation. Some people are too proud or have too big an ego to ask for help until it's too late.

How can I personally help you turn around your financial picture and reach your goals?

I provide online coaching and training, live group sessions, workshops, and customized company training. I also offer personal coaching. My goal is to help turn around families and companies struggling with financial stress. After using these techniques and creating a solid financial plan, you'll feel more confident. You'll also notice that your worry and stress levels decrease.

I have other options, but these are great for saving your money. They help you stretch every dollar of your income right now. They will help provide some quick financial relief.

Share this with your family, friends, and coworkers.

This way, they can receive these tips and sign up for my list to get more as soon as I publish them. Go to www.FinancialReliefCoach.com to get a free e-book and get on my list.

Give me a call or e-mail to learn more:

Jeff Wilson
Financial Relief University
Toledo, Ohio
Ph #419-842-8112
E-mail: Jeff@LifesCheatSheets.com

Now go take action today and get these techniques working for you and your family!

P.S. For more financial and success tips, visit www.LifesCheatSheets.com to check out my #1 Best Seller. Jump on Amazon and get a copy for yourself. Alternatively, contact me and I can send you a signed copy. It provides success tips that you typically don't learn in school.

About Jeff

"Street Cred"

Jeff grew up in Fayette, Ohio, a small town with just one stoplight 35 miles west of Toledo, Ohio. He was and continues to be a very driven person, letting little stop him once he sets his mind to something. Having bought his first rental home at a sheriff's auction as a 17-year old high school senior in the 80's, he rarely does the "normal" thing.

For over 30 years since high school (15 of those while in college outside of work hours), Jeff ran, owned, turned around, and sold companies. He filled the roles of CFO, COO, CEO, In-House Counsel, and Turnaround Specialist, helping those companies reach record sales and profits several years. He also provided financial planning services, served on multiple boards, and volunteered and did pro bono work for over 25 entities. Jeff taught at three colleges and has given estate and financial planning seminars. Having consulted with a number of companies, led and assisted with start-ups, company growth, and business turnarounds, he is now sharing some of the wisdom gained from all of his unique experiences.

Jeff has a long list of credentials, including JD (licensed attorney in Ohio & Michigan), MBA, MHA, CMA, CBM, BS, and AA in management, marketing, computer science, finance, and law. He also completed advanced training in real estate investing, was a Realtor and auctioneer, and obtained Series 7 & 66 securities licenses as well as insurance/annuities licenses. As a real estate investor, he remains active in foreclosure/bank-owned (REO), bankruptcy, and probate properties, self-storage facilities, and mobile home/RV parks. Jeff has played competitive volleyball, pickleball, and golf, and emcees and sings at local events. He regularly spends time with his wife, Beth, family, and Bichon-Maltese little buddies.

His #1 Best-Seller book series called Life's Cheat Sheets: Crucial Success Habits School Never Taught You inspires readers to develop real-life street-smart skills that are vital for success. It shows them how to control their mind, think big, and take daily action to achieve their dreams (www.LifesCheatSheets.com).

Jeff is also the founder of a related brand called Financial Relief University (www.FinancialReliefU.com). This book focuses on reducing and controlling expenses while subsequent books in this series will focus more on income streams, additional expense reductions, emergency fund, paying off debt, and investments. He has a companion workbook published for this book on Amazon that is very helpful in completing the tasks laid out herein. The series is focused on turning around families' financial pictures, like he did with companies, which reduces stress on the family.

Next in the Financial Relief Series

Future Plans

Besides looking at adding an e-book/Kindle version, an audio book, an online course, personal coaching, and possibly a membership site, blog, or podcast, I have plans for more books in this series. They will help readers take several steps further to improve their future. Feel free to write and tell me what would help you best in this list of options.

Potential Topics for More Books and Courses in this Series:

Simplified Financial Plan Concept
More comparison shopping
Strategic negotiating
New-Extra income options
Additional ways to reduce expenses
Minimizing travel costs
Emergency fund
Paying off all debt
ROI vs. Expense concept
Power of compounding

Simple investment options
Diversifying investments

Active investing
Dollar cost average investing
Roth & IRA investing
Equity-Stocks, ETFs, Mutual Funds
Bonds
Annuities
Refining your plan
Short-term, mid-term, long-term planning

Basic estate planning
Wills, Powers of Attorney, Healthcare directives
Direct distributions via beneficiary designations
Avoiding probate
Revocable Living Trusts
Specific devises
Detailed distribution directions
Long term care
Life insurance needs

Go to my site (www.FinancialReliefCoach.com) and sign up for my email list, plus you'll get my free e-book. You will get the earliest notification once new information is published.

Please e-mail me with other topics you would like to see included in the series at Jeff@lifescheatsheets.com.

Thank You

I appreciate your following and feedback

I want to express my gratitude for choosing and purchasing my book and/or workbook. In a world overflowing with choices, you selected mine, and for that, I'm truly thankful.

Before we part ways, may I request a minor favor? I would love for you to leave a review on the Amazon platform. For an independent author like myself, receiving direct reader feedback through reviews significantly contributes to the success of the work and keeps me publishing more.

Your insights will guide me in creating content that effectively aids you in achieving your desired results. Your feedback is highly valuable to me.

Thank you for your time and consideration.

I personally read every one to hear what meant the most to each reader.

All you have to do is search for and bring up my book listing on Amaz on.com, scroll down to Customer Reviews, then Write a Review on what you liked most.

Thanks again,

Jeff Wilson

Endnotes

1. LendingClub. 2025. "Nearly 60% of Credit Cardholders in the U.S. Live Paycheck to Paycheck." LendingClub Insights. February. Accessed July 1 2025.

2. Frugalwoods. 2015. "Banish Debt Like a Boss: Demystifying Personal Finance Part 2." Frugalwoods, March 11, 2015. Accessed July 1, 2025.

3. Intuit. 2023. "Survey: 65 % of Americans Don't Know How Much They Spent Last Month." *Intuit Financial Insights*, 2023. Accessed July 1, 2025.

4. ValuePenguin. 2023. "How Credit Cards Affect Spending Habits." ValuePenguin. Last modified March 8, 2023. Accessed July 1, 2025. https://www.valuepenguin.com/credit-cards/credit-card-spending-studies.

5. Federal Reserve Bank of St. Louis. 2024. "Which U.S. Households Have Credit Card Debt?" On the Economy, May 2024. Accessed July 1, 2025.

6. Prelec, Drazen, and Sachin Banker. 2021. "MIT Sloan Study Shows Credit Cards Act to 'Step on the Gas' to Increase Spending." MIT Sloan School of Management. March 11, 2021. Accessed July 2, 2025.

7. American Automobile Association. 2024. "Your Driving Costs: The Price of New Car Ownership." AAA Newsroom, September 2024. Accessed July 2, 2025.

8. KFF (via PeopleKeep). 2023. "Average Family Health Insurance Costs $23,968 per Year." PeopleKeep. Accessed July 2 2025.

9. Commonwealth Fund. 2024. "State of Health Insurance Coverage in the U.S.: 2024 Biennial Survey." Commonwealth Fund, November 2024. Accessed July 2 2025.

10. USAFacts. 2025. "How Many Households in the United States Spend Too Much on Housing?" USAFacts, January 29, 2025. Accessed July 2, 2025.

11. Education Data Initiative. 2025. "Student Loan Debt Statistics." Education Data Initiative, March 16, 2025. Accessed July 3, 2025.

12. TIME. 2024. "Negotiate for Lower Bills With These Expert Tips." TIME, June 28, 2024. Accessed July 3, 2025.

Instant Order Form

Feel free to call in the order

PRESTIGE PUBLISHING
INSTANT ORDER FORM

Order Date: ______________________

Name: ______________________

Address: ______________________

City/State/Zip: ______________________

Telephone: ______________________

Email Address: ______________________

Phone Orders: 1-866-475-4675 or 1-419-842-8112
Email Orders: Jeff@lifescheatsheets.com

Please send the following books/materials:

____

____

____

We will contact you for payment information once we receive this order or you may order it direct from Amazon.com.

*We will add 7.75% sales tax to orders shipped to Ohio addresses
*Shipping is approximately $4.00 for the first book

Please send me additional information on the following items: (circle)

Speaking Coaching Consulting

Publishing Partnership Volume Purchase

Made in the USA
Monee, IL
04 November 2026

67377189R00085